This is the lively, engrossing guide that I wish I had when I was an isolated country boy writing and drawing my own comics. Now young creators can see that there are more opportunities and outlets than ever to tell and share their stories. This book is a great how-to primer on comics for kids—or an entry-level introduction to the form and the industry for anyone who wonders how comics are put together.

—**Phil Simon**, editor, Dark Horse Comics

I love the range of guidance given to kids but also the range of "real" artists who contribute to the book. Their varied styles and degrees of sophistication make room for all sorts of dreamers. It is a rich resource for aspiring comics artists.

—**Dr. Carol Ann Tomlinson**, author of *The Differentiated Classroom*

Phil Amara takes his personal experience in the comics industry, adds his passion for teaching, and cooks up a delicious recipe for creating one's very own comic book! *So, You Want to Be a Comic Book Artist?* is a wonderful introduction into the exciting journey of creating and understanding sequential art.

—**Keith Wood**, art director, Oni Press

What Phil Amara has accomplished here is a sort of magic act: an illuminating guide to a mysterious career.

—**Adam Gallardo**, comics writer, *Star Wars: Infinities, Gear School, 100 Girls*

Praise for *So, You Want to Be a Comic Book Ar*

The straightforward text and the structure
the presentation could make *So, You Want*
Be a Comic Book Artist? the standard for teachi
comics in school.

—Jon Bogdanove, acclaimed Superman artis

So, You Want to Be a Comic Book Artist? is everything the ten-year-old me wanted!
Perfect for daydreamers, four-color optimists, and doers of daring deeds, this book
will give kids and kids-at-heart the tools to make their imaginations soar. Insightful
and accessible, Amara has created more than just a how-to book, it's a love letter
to a truly American art form—comics!

—Matthew Cody, author of *Powerless*

So, You Want to Be a Comic Book Artist? is smart, fun, and insightful. I highly
recommend it for anyone who has ever dreamed of becoming a comic book artist.

—Jim Hardison, comics writer, *The Helm*

Any young cartoonist dreaming of breaking into the field of comics and graphic
novels must have this book! It's a treasure trove of useful information and solid
cartooning principles and practices. Understanding and developing story ideas and
plot, creating characters, laying out pages, self-publishing, understanding the comics publishing business, and interviews with novice and professional cartoonists—I
wish I had this book when I was a kid! Parents will find this a valuable resource
to promote their child's burgeoning interest in this exciting career. And teachers will find this an invaluable resource for their students' self-directed learning
opportunities.

—Richard Jenkins, author of *Comics in Your Curriculum*

SO, YOU WANT TO BE A COMIC BOOK ARTIST?

THE ULTIMATE GUIDE ON HOW TO BREAK INTO COMICS!

PHILIP AMARA

ALADDIN
New York London Toronto Sydney New Delhi

BEYOND WORDS
Hillsboro, Oregon

ALADDIN
An imprint of Simon & Schuster
Children's Publishing Division
1230 Avenue of the Americas
New York, NY 10020

BEYOND WORDS
20827 N.W. Cornell Road, Suite 500
Hillsboro, Oregon 97124-9808
503-531-8700 / 503-531-8773 fax
www.beyondword.com

This Aladdin/Beyond Words edition September 2012
Copyright © 2001, 2009, 2012 by Philip Amara
Previously published as *So, You Wanna Be a Comic Book Artist?*

For information about special discounts for bulk purchases, please contact Simon & Schuster Special Sales at 1-866-506-1949 or business@simonandschuster.com.

The Simon & Schuster Speakers Bureau can bring authors to your live event. For more information or to book an event contact the Simon & Schuster Speakers Bureau at 1-866-248-3049 or visit our website at www.simonspeakers.com.

Managing Editor: Lindsay S. Brown
Designer: Sara E. Blum
Copyeditors: Emmalisa Sparrow, Kristin Thiel
Proofreader: Michelle Blair
The text of this book was set in Bembo.

Manufactured in the United States of America 0812 FFG

10 9 8 7 6 5 4 3 2 1

Library of Congress Cataloging-in-Publication Data

Amara, Philip.
    So, you want to be a comic book artist? / written by Philip Amara.
        — [Updated edition].
        pages   cm
    Includes bibliographical references.
    1. Comic books, strips, etc.—Authorship—Juvenile literature. 2. Comic
        books, strips, etc.—Technique—Juvenile literature. [1. Cartoons and comics-
        Authorship—Juvenile literature.] I. Title.
    PN6710.A59   2012
    741.5'1—dc23

2011050715

ISBN 978-1-58270-357-2 (pbk)
ISBN 978-1-58270-358-9 (hc)
ISBN 978-1-4424-5717-1 (eBook)

ACKNOWLEDGMENTS

Thanks: Ben Abernathy, Dave Bullock, Alina Chau, Caroline Chatelet, Mark Chiarello, Eddie Choi, Adam Gallardo, Shaenon Garrity, Sarah Gaydos, Tom Hart, Toru Hashizumi, Rich Jenkins, Beth Kawasaki, Lance Krieter, Gary Larson for inventing the word *thagomizer*, Raymond Leslie, Aki Matsunobu, Pop Mhan, Kaitlin Mischner, Jack Pollock, Phil Simon, Joshua Izzo, Brandon Vietti, Keith Wood, Jim Zubkavich, Lindsay Brown, Jenefer Angell, Jen Weaver-Neist, Emmalisa Sparrow, Sara Blum, Cynthia Black, and Richard Cohn.

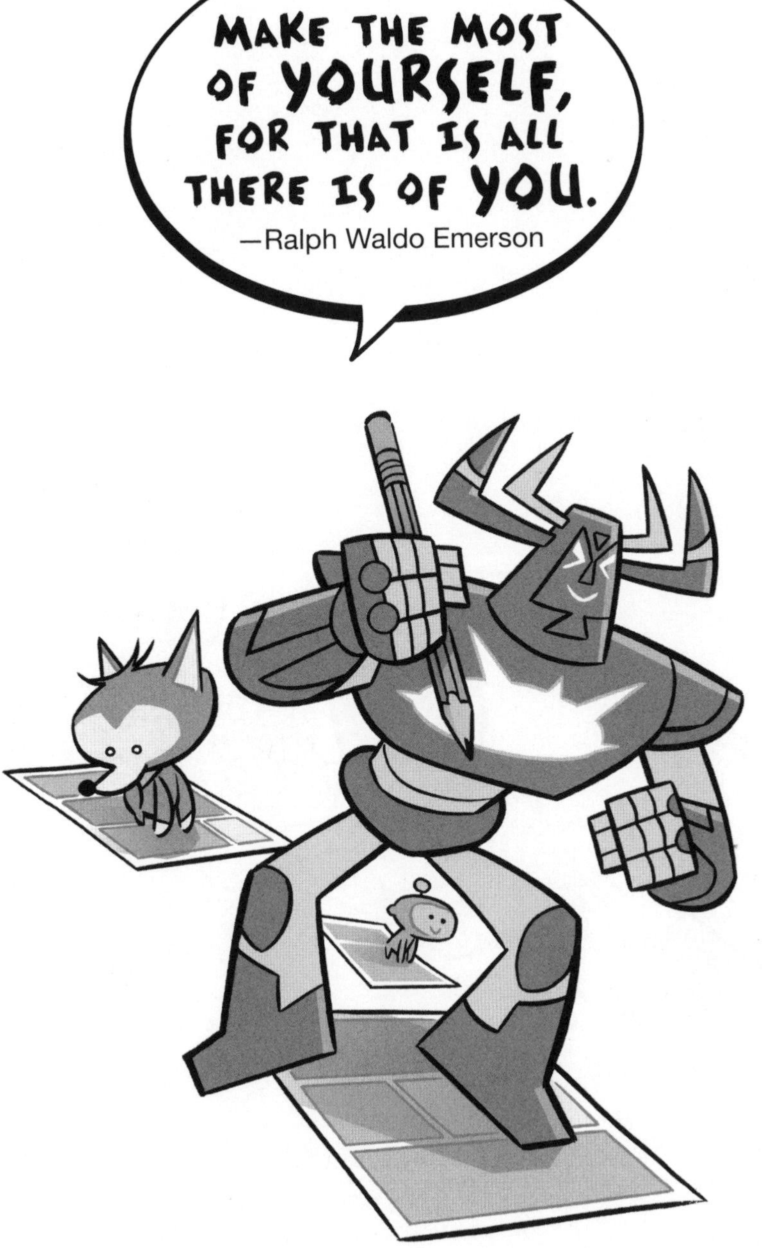
MAKE THE MOST OF YOURSELF, FOR THAT IS ALL THERE IS OF YOU.
—Ralph Waldo Emerson

CONTENTS

INTRODUCTION

If you're a lifelong comics fan like me, you already know that one-of-a-kind feeling you get when you walk into a comic book store—if you're lucky, on a Wednesday: new-release day—and new comics are on the shelves. As a kid, I spent my Saturdays at a store called The Million Year Picnic in Cambridge, near Boston. There, I flipped through back issues and spent my allowance on *Daredevil*, *Thor*, *Fantastic Four*, *Teen Titans*, and *Batman*. I'm sure you have your favorites, too.

By the time I was in college, I was writing articles about my favorite comics for comics magazines and local newspapers. I even started a comics radio show and interviewed famous comics creators like Stan Lee and Jack Kirby, two true icons of Marvel Comics. Eventually, this hobby led to a decade-long career in comics. Now I'm a schoolteacher in Boston, and I get to pass on my love of comics to my students. We actually have comics class!

Many comics fans dream of becoming comic book artists—but how do you do that? In your hands is a guide to creating your own comics *right now*. It covers a variety of interests and abilities. Each chapter has information to help you become a comic book artist. You'll read advice from comics pros like Bryan Lee O'Malley, well-known for *Scott Pilgrim*, and Art Baltazar, artist of *Patrick the Wolf Boy*. (Some of the other artists interviewed in this book have even used comics to help prepare them for other careers.) Plus, a few young comic book artists will give their advice. In this book, jump around to see what catches your interest and what helps you the most.

You'll also see characters like the one below to spotlight comics info and trivia:

Whether you're starting out or have been drawing comics for years, remember this: *Anyone can create comics.* You don't have to wait until you're older. You don't need fancy equipment. Use your comics to comment on who you are and what the world around you is like. Comics are pretty powerful. Only *you* can tell *your* story *your* way.

SO, YOU WANT TO BE A COMIC BOOK ARTIST?

You are sitting at your very own table at a comics convention. Behind you is a huge sign with your name written across it. Everything is quiet and seems to be moving in slo-mo. Suddenly—CRACK!—the doors at the end of the hall burst open, and a huge crowd of people rushes in, straight toward you. They all want you to sign the latest copy of your comic book creation. Some of them are even dressed up as your characters!

"Wow," you think as you whip out your pen and begin signing, "This is unreal, dude."

Have you ever imagined creating your own comic? With just a few tools and materials, a little guidance, some effort, and a whole bunch of imagination, you can!

I attend comic book conventions whenever I can. Artist friends send me samples of their work for feedback. As a young artist who's just starting out in comics, you'll want to have someone look at your work. It might be a brother or sister, a friend, or a teacher. Eventually, you'll have the chance to show your work to comics professionals, and they'll want to see that your love of comics shines on the page.

COMICS: A WORK OF ART?

Your parents may threaten to throw your comics in the trash, but you guard them with your life and make your friends swear to keep them in mint condition whenever they borrow them. Sound familiar? Even in the days of downloads and apps, comics fans still like to buy, read, and collect the genuine article right from our local comics shops. As with all forms of art, comics are looked at in different ways by different kinds of people. Some people (not me or you!) consider comics to be a low form of art. Others pay lots of money to collect rare issues of popular comics. It all depends on how you look at it.

Art historians often classify comics as *pop art* (short for *popular art*). Pop art is found everywhere in modern culture and mass media: in computer-rendered art for video games, cartoons, Japanese animated movies (*anime*), magazine illustrations, comic strips, and advertisements.

Did you ever think that you could change the world with a comic book? Just because comics are considered pop art doesn't mean that you can't make a serious statement with them. Some comics are so good that you could claim them as fine art or literature. Countless comic book artists have been recognized and awarded for groundbreaking achievements. Comics have their own language, just like music and film, for conveying emotion, theme, style, and story. They can persuade, entertain, and inform. And just like music and film, comics have the ability to transform the way people think.

If you're going to be a comic book artist, it's important to know that comic books are a form of sequential art. This definition includes graphic novels, *manga* (Japanese comic books), and comic strips. In this book, I'll often refer to all these forms of sequential art as comics, but it's helpful to understand some differences between them.

Comic books: You know what they are when you see them—*Superman*, *Thor*, *Bakuman*, and the list goes on. But, if you want to get technical, comic books come in every style and format you can imagine. Traditional comic books are usually twenty-two to thirty-two pages long and about 6½ inches wide by 10½ inches high, but this can vary a little ... or a lot. Some comic books are oversize magazines that stretch tall, while others are tiny and more horizontal. Some take years to complete, and some are done in twenty-four hours.

Comic strips: Though we get our news by computer more and more each day, you should still know what a comic strip is. They're usually just a few panels long, in a horizontal format, and tell a quick story or joke. Some famous comic strips are *Calvin and Hobbes* and *Peanuts*. Years ago, comic strips like *Little Nemo in Slumberland*, *Prince Valiant*, and *Tarzan* took up a whole page in the newspaper. Nowadays, we'd probably call those web comics or eComics, and they might never be published on paper. If you go to a comics publisher's website, you can usually find plenty of eComics in lots of different genres and art styles. It's great inspiration.

> Sequential art, a.k.a. comics, is a series of repetitious drawings of characters that are used to tell a story. There's a passage of time, and a beginning, middle, and end. Will Eisner uses the phrase in his book *Comics and Sequential Art* (W. W. Norton, 2008).

Graphic novels: Typically, squarebound comics close

to or over one hundred pages are called graphic novels (or trade paperbacks). They focus on one story or main character. Sometimes this is a collection of a bunch of comics in one book, and sometimes it's an original book all by itself. Koge-Donbo's *Kamichama Karin* ran in a magazine called *Nakayoshi* before it was made into collections. Craig Thompson's 672-page *Habibi* was originally published all at once in book form. Don't drop that one on your foot!

Zines: Zines are inexpensively produced, self-published publications. The best part about zines is that they can cover just about anything—your zine can include everything from comics, articles, and reviews to poetry and photos. Because zines are so cheap to make, they are a great way to showcase your talents, get feedback on your work from friends, and experiment with new ideas.

Manga: *Manga* means "comic" in Japanese. Manga characters can be magical creatures, pets, sports teams, or ordinary kids off on an extraordinary adventure. Sometimes manga are split into *shonen* (for boys) and *shojo* (for girls) in a Japanese comic shop, but you can read what you like, of course. Some of the most popular manga, like *Naruto*, *Fullmetal Alchemist*, *One Piece*, and *Case Closed* starring Detective Conan, have become animated series in Japan and around the world.

BRYAN LEE O'MALLEY

From: London, Ontario, Canada
Job: Full-time cartoonist
His Comic: *Scott Pilgrim*

What was your first or favorite comic when you were younger?

My favorite comic was *X-Men*! I started reading it in grade five and would read it on and off through high school. It had a lot of imagination and the most compelling characters. It felt like it took place in a real, vibrant, exciting world.

Scott Pilgrim © Bryan Lee O'Malley

Kim Pine © Bryan Lee O'Malley

When did you know you wanted to make comics?

I always made comics. I still have comics from when I was three years old (my mom saved them). I really never considered doing anything else, except a brief period when I wanted to be a "real writer" when I was about seventeen to eighteen. I even used to make comics for school assignments whenever my teachers would allow it.

What kinds of things inspire your comic book creations?
Everything! Books (fiction and nonfiction), comics (especially old, weird Japanese ones), movies, music, video games, friends, family, life, walking down the street.

What tools do you use to create your comics?
I use a mix of computer stuff and old-school stuff. Lately I do my sketching on the computer, then print it out and finish it up using a very old-school technique: dipping a brush in ink. It seems like something from long ago, and it took me a long time to learn, but I really like how it looks.

What are great ways for kids to create comics right now?
The great thing about comics is that you can use any tool that happens to be lying around. When I was a kid, I used markers, pencil crayons, ballpoint pens, lined paper, the margins of my school notes, whatever was around. The great thing about being a kid is you have plenty of time to draw during class! Don't tell anyone I told you that.

How do you use technology to create comics?
Like I said, I've been sketching on the computer lately. I have a tablet pen. It makes sketching easy, because you can correct mistakes in a snap. It seems to free my mind from worry.

Why is telling a story with comics important to you?
I think comics are the best! They're cheap and quick to produce, and it's a great way to get ideas directly out of your head and into the world. You can tell any kind of story you want, and your characters can be anything. There are no limits except your imagination. When I was a kid, my friends and I would make comics just to make each other laugh. Now I try to make lots of people laugh.

GOOD COMICS

Making a good comic is like making a delicious pizza: There are a few essential ingredients, and each one has a specific role. A pizza is a pizza because it has a crust, sauce, and cheese, and comics have certain ingredients that make them comics: panels, balloons, and captions, to name a few. If you mix these ingredients together in the right balance, you'll end up with an intriguing comic. If you leave out one or two of the major ingredients, it will show in the final product. The basic ingredients for a cool comic go a little something like this:

Panels: Panels are the squares or rectangles of art in a comic that give your story structure. Each panel shows some kind of progression in your story, and that's what makes a comic sequential. Panels can be of any size or shape as long as the art fits inside. Often, there are about six panels per page. Though you don't *have* to use panels to tell a comics story, most comic book illustrators use them to distinguish one scene from the next. Andi Watson's comic *Glister* sometimes uses characters, like a snake, to frame the panel. A cool trick, and it gives the story another layer, too.

Gutters: The gutters are the white margins around a page's edge and the white spaces between the panels. Usually panels don't butt up against each other or go right to the edge of the page. When they do go to the edge of a page, it's called a *bleed*.

Balloons: Not hot-air balloons. Not birthday balloons. Word balloons illustrate characters' conversations, loud noises, and thoughts. Comics artists usually keep the number of words per balloon small—twenty-five to forty. New artists sometimes fill their panels with so much art, there's no room for balloons, so remember to leave a little space. Think of a panel like your room at home. You have space for your extravagant solar-powered jetpack and your rocket-fueled surfboard... but is there also room for essentials like a school backpack, winter clothes, a desk, and a bed?

Captions: Captions are like balloons. They help tell the story, but they usually do not show you the conversation between characters. They are rectangular or square in shape and typically hold a narrator's words, describe a scene, or establish a time period in the comic. They're the spaces the comics writer uses to add info to the story instead of Batman or *Diary of a Wimpy Kid*'s Greg Heffley talking. Sometimes captions are used for a flashback, when one of the characters is remembering events that happened already.

Title: The title is what you're going to call your comic. Try to pick a title that gives the reader a hint about the comic, but leaves them wanting more as well. If you name your comic *Summer Camp Superheroes*, you want a fan to be asking, "What's a Summer Camp Superhero?" Then, you want that person to flip through your comic and join your characters on their adventures. Some people title their comics after their main character, like *Superman*. Marvel Comics likes to add an adjective, like *The Mighty Thor*, *The Uncanny X-Men*, and *The Invincible Iron Man*. Your comic book title can

A comics character's first appearance isn't always in his own book. Superman debuted in *Action Comics* #1, and Batman in *Detective Comics* #27. Spider-Man first appeared in *Amazing Fantasy* #15, and Iron Man in *Tales of Suspense* #39.

appear anywhere on the cover, but it's usually in the top-third portion, or tier, of the page.

The X factor: There's one more ingredient you'll need to create an extraordinary comic: imagination. It's the X factor—the magic you and you alone bring to a story—that's going to make it memorable. What makes the *Harry Potter*, *Percy Jackson*, and *Star Wars* films and books so amazing? It's not just the special effects or the actors, but the auteur behind it—the person with a deliberate, creative vision. Just like J. K. Rowling, Rick Riordan, and George Lucas, you're going to be the auteur behind your comic. How you execute your story and work with the comic book ingredients is what's going to set your masterpiece apart.

THE WORLD OF COMICS AWAITS YOU

Okay, you've decided that you enjoy reading comics so much that you want to create some of your own. You have dozens of ideas for characters and stories bursting like popcorn in your head. You've started to doodle or sketch some of these characters on scraps of paper. This is just the beginning! You're about to start your own studio, learn about the tools of the trade, and get some important hints for creating your stories. You're entering the exciting world of comics, and there's no turning back!

ALEXIS CORNELL

Age: 19
Education: Undergraduate student at The Center for Cartoon Studies
Her Comic: untitled

What are your favorite comic books?

Three books that I would suggest to anyone, anytime—justification being "you have to read this it's SO GOOD"—are *Serenity Rose*, *Muhyo and Roji's Bureau of Supernatural Investigations*, and *Bone*. I like to read long stories that focus on the characters, especially if they're set in a cool, well-built world.

Why do you like creating comics?

I love to write stories, and I love to draw. Put those together, and you get comics! I think you get the closest to the creator's vision of their world and characters through comics, which is really cool.

Where do you get the inspiration for your creations?

Mostly while listening to music or taking long walks outside, but inspiration is all over the place! Inspiration is a funny thing in that it can hit you anywhere, anytime, and it especially likes the shower when there's no paper around.

What are your favorite tools to use when writing and drawing comics?

Piles of notebooks, mechanical pencils in .05 and .07 leads, and my favorite nibs. G-nibs, crow quills, and globe quills are my weapons of choice, but recently I've been working on getting better with a brush. For paper, I use smooth Bristol (preferably recycled). And tea! Lots of herbal teas. That's totally a tool.

RECENTLY, I'VE BEEN FEELING LIKE I'M NEGLECTING MY OWN STORIES AND CHARACTERS.

DRAW US LEX!

DRAW US!

BUT GUYS, HOMEWORK...

Poof

IT'S NOT LIKE I'VE FORGOTTEN ABOUT THEM, IT'S JUST THAT I'VE BEEN STARTING ALL OF OUR ASSIGNMENTS WITH A CLEAN SLATE.

SCHOOL

ANTHOLOGY

DIARIES

BIBLIOMANCY

HEY!

SCHOOLS

← SERIOUS COMICS FACE

So STARTING NOW, MY DIARIES ARE GONNA BE ABOUT MY OWN STUFF.

DRAW UUUSSSS

GUYS NO--

DO ITTT

PUT US IN COMICS!

COME ONNNN

WE MISS YOU

I DUNNO HOW MUCH I CAN GET DONE, BUT AT LEAST IT'LL BE SOMETHING.

FINE.

YAAAA AAAAYY

Does technology help you create?

I do as much as I can (which is most things) on paper, but sometimes there are effects you can only get with a computer, and if you mess up a panel so badly you can't fix it on the original paper, you can redraw it on a separate piece, and just drop it in on the computer.

How do you think making comics could help you in other creative careers?

Comics are actually used in many different jobs. When you plot out a TV show or a movie, it's done through thumbnails, just like in comics! Or if you're a scrapbooker, making comics will teach you about page layouts and design, which both carry over into your scrapbook.

What are your plans for the future?

I'd like to get my stories out there and maybe even have people like them! Best case scenario (and the one I'm shooting for) is to be able to survive solely on my comics and draw them for the rest of my life. That's a dream come true.

What's the best advice you can give your peers?

Write EVERYTHING down, even the silly ideas you come up with at 3 AM. Keep a notebook by your bed. Don't ever tell yourself, "Oh, I'm not good enough to do this story yet." Just do it! And if you end up in a creative-mess-everything-I-do-is-terrible-art slump, plow your way through it! Tell yourself that you are awesome, and everything you do is awesome, and ride that wave of awesome right out of that art block.

STARTING A STUDIO
AND THE TOOLS OF
THE TRADE

You are trying to draw an incredible alien character that just popped into your head, but your blue ballpoint pen isn't doing the trick. Some leftover potato chips keep getting on the paper, making everything greasy and gross.

"Aaargh!" you yell and crumple up your drawing, throwing it on the floor with the others. You look around your room at the mess. You can't seem to draw anything in this messy place!

If you're going to be a comic book artist, you will need artist supplies that support both your precision (the focus you put into your comics) and your expression (the ideas you put into your comics). This chapter contains all the information you need to set yourself up to create fantastic comics.

MY STUDIO—KEEP OUT!

Before you do any drawing, writing, sketching, or inking, you'll need to put together a studio, a place where you can do your best work. Your studio doesn't have to be a stuffy private study, or an expensive artist's loft—you can transform a section of your room, or turn a tabletop into a working studio. You can make a mobile studio and take it with you.

The first step to creating your own studio is to find a space that offers some privacy and where you feel comfortable drawing. Let your family know that this is your private work area and, if possible, not to disturb you while you're there. Once you've established an ideal location for your studio, check to make sure you have the following crucial studio items.

WARNING: Be careful not to turn your studio into a game cave: no television, video games, cell phones, frozen pizzas, or cheese nachos. This is not a hangout. This is your oasis for creating your own comics—embrace its *productive* atmosphere.

Drawing table or desk: One of the most important features of your studio should be a good place to draw. Any kind of flat, sturdy surface will do: a card table, kitchen table (you might want to wipe it off first), countertop, desk, or folding table. You can even buy a portable drawing board at an art supply store, or make one with pieces of wood. Try to avoid drawing while lying down on the floor. It's tempting, but it won't give your arm a proper range of motion.

Art supplies: Every comics artist uses different artistic supplies, but a standard toolkit includes pens, brushes, and paper.

16

See the "Tools of the Trade" section of this chapter for more on the supplies you'll need. (The profiled artists have some info, too.)

Light: If your studio has a window, that's great, but a table lamp or two with bulbs around seventy-five watts are essential so that you can see well for detailed drawing and inking (coloring in). At some point, you might want to invest in a quality, swiveling desk lamp.

A comfy chair: Finding a chair with good back support is extremely important. With a comfortable chair, you can withstand hours of drawing comics. A cushion or pillow on the chair's seat will help as well. It might sound silly now, but after drawing for a few hours, you'll see what I mean. Take a stretch break once in a while, too.

Snacks (optional): Snacks can be great while working and can energize your creativity and let you keep working when you might otherwise be distracted by a rumbly stomach. When you need some extra inspiration, an oatmeal cookie or a banana can go a long way! Just be sure any snacks are a safe distance from your most prized artwork. Do I need to say it? No hot fudge sundaes.

Tunes (optional): Music that inspires you can help you focus or even stimulate the creative process. Choose whatever music you like and that also gets your creative juices flowing. Try different kinds to see what works best for you. Styles to try might be as different as hip-hop, country, rock, R&B, freakbeat, techno, reggaeton, and classical.

Decorations (optional): Posters by your favorite artists or pages from your favorite comics hung on the walls of your studio can help motivate your creativity. Even better, hang some photos of facial expressions, poses, and everyday things (cars, planes, dogs, trees, sandwiches, boots, hats, clouds) to fuel the characters and places in your comics.

What's in a name: Give your studio a name and logo that expresses your own unique style—for example, Top Dog Studio, Monster's Ink, Paper Weight, or Creation Station. If your studio name is Top Dog, draw a dog with a confident attitude for your logo. Make a studio sign and hang it on your door or put it near your drawing table whenever you're working. Having a logo will let your friends know you mean business. Mountain Dew wouldn't be the same if it was just Sweet Green Liquid. Give people a name and a comic they'll remember.

For more than four billion dollars in 2009, Disney purchased Marvel Comics and their catalog of five-thousand-plus characters. Disney also owns ABC-TV, ESPN, and Pixar.

Studio ... to go: If you go away on vacation and you want to draw, make up a portable version of your studio. Put pens, pencils, and a sketchbook in a box (old lunch boxes from thrift stores work great, and they're cheap) or a plastic ziplock bag, so your work will be protected from the elements. You can also pack a hard, but lightweight, drawing surface if you think you'll need one. A laptop, computer tablet, or smartphone is handy for doing art research, but really, all you need is something to draw *with* and something to draw *on*.

Have fun while you work. Unlike doing homework or chores, with drawing comics, you have the freedom to do as little or as much as you want, whenever you want. Your success is totally up to you. But remember: Success takes time and dedication, so it's important to develop good drawing habits.

Start by going to your studio every other day for just ten to fifteen minutes. Chances are you'll have so much fun drawing that you'll stay there longer anyway. When you're ready, try to devote more time to drawing daily, maybe forty-five minutes to an hour. Before you know it, that hour will go by as quickly as the very first fifteen minutes!

TOOLS OF THE TRADE

If you really want to create great comics, you're going to require some basic drawing tools and supplies. You don't need to buy fancy art supplies—a few pencils, some pens, and an artist sketchpad will work great. You're here to draw and create, not to worry about using some superpen, forged from a mysterious asteroid. Let's face it, if you really had to, you could draw with a stick in the sand. The tools are important, but not as much as the ideas in your head and your willingness to express them.

Any good art store will provide one-stop shopping for pens, brushes, paper, and pencils. You might want to check out the following items once you're there.

PAPER

The first sketchbook I bought was expensive, had a nice binding and a thick cover . . . and I was terrified to use it! I thought everything I sketched in it had to be good enough for a museum. When I finally tried drawing on a cheap block of newsprint, I couldn't fill it fast enough, and I got better much faster. The list below offers some helpful tips on how to find the best paper for your drawing desires.

> **Paper weight:** Most papers come in different weights—twenty pound, thirty pound, and fifty pound. This doesn't mean that one sheet of paper weighs fifty pounds (yikes!). The weight refers to how much a box of that particular paper

Elisabetta Gnone, Alessandro Barbucci, and Barbara Canepa's Italian comic *W.I.T.C.H.* spawned English-language adaptations, manga, an animated series, and a Gameboy video game.

weighs. If you're sketching, light paper, like newsprint, is probably the best. But if you're producing finished art, you may want to use thicker paper that weighs more.

Newsprint: Small newsprint sketchpads work great for getting any initial ideas down on paper. You don't even have to go to an art supply store to get one. They're usually available in the stationery aisle of your supermarket. Try a hundred-sheet pad of 6-by-9 inch recycled newsprint for both pencil and charcoal drawings. They come in 9-by-12 inch sizes, too, at the local art store.

Sketchpad: If you're using pencils and charcoal a lot, you might want to look into a sketchpad. Try a hundred-sheet pad of fifty-pound, 11-by-14 inch recycled paper. It has a slightly rough surface and is more durable than newsprint.

Drawing pad: Sometimes "sketch" paper is labeled "drawing" paper. The main difference is that drawing paper is heavier (eighty pound) than paper in a standard sketchpad. Try a twenty-four-sheet pad of fourteen-by-seventeen-inch Strathmore regular surface. Most are labeled "acid-free," which means they won't discolor over time like newsprint. Good acid-free brands of sketch paper are Strathmore, Aquabee, and Canson.

Bristol board: Most professional comic book artists use Bristol board, but it's not cheap ($10 for about twenty sheets).

You may want to stick to less expensive paper—a sketchpad you can feel comfortable filling with an explosion of ideas *and* that you won't have to worry about ruining because of the cost. Bristol board does have its advantages, however: It's durable and acid free, and the size is proportionate to most comics pages. If you're interested in trying Bristol board, look for a twenty-sheet pad of 11-by-14 inch Strathmore, one hundred pound, with a smooth finish. Smooth Bristol is what most comics artists prefer because ink works well with the surface. Coarse Bristol (also called vellum) works well for dry media, like soft pencils and charcoal, but you can ink on it, too.

PENS, PENCILS—AND TOOTHBRUSHES?!

Even unexpected things, like an old toothbrush, can be transformed into drawing tools. Many professional comics artists not only use typical tools like pencils, pens, and brushes but also use unorthodox tools. These tools offer different levels of flexibility, reliability, and effect.

As you try these different tools, it's a good idea to experiment and see what works best for you. Keep in mind that not all experiments yield good results. My pal Tony Millionaire, creator of *Sock Monkey*, said, "Once, I lost my favorite pen and had to do an illustration with a black Bic. It was pretty bad." Check out this list of tools, both traditional and

Different artists try different tools. Alex Maleev likes toothbrushes for a splatter effect. Pop Mhan sometimes uses Q-tips to put flat, smooth ink on the page. Award-winner Mark Schultz is well known for his masterful dry-brush technique.

odd, that you can find anywhere—from your local hardware store to the art-supply websites listed at the back of this book.

ELEANOR DAVIS

From: Tucson, Arizona
Job: Freelance artist
Her Comics: *The Secret Science Alliance and the Copycat Crook,*
Stinky, **and self-published mini-comics**

What was your first or favorite comic when you were younger?
I have a very long list. At the top would be *Little Lulu* and the Carl Barks's duck comics.

When did you know you wanted to make comics?
I've drawn comics off and on since I was very small—before I can remember. I got really serious about it during my teens, however.

What kinds of things inspire your comic book creations?
Everything! For my kid comics, I just try to put myself back to when I was a kid and think of the most fun, exciting stuff I can possibly imagine.

What tools do you use to create your comics?
I use lots of different tools when making different comics. I usually use Strathmore 400 Series Bristol to draw on, Higgins's or Dr. Ph. Martin's Bombay black ink, and a dip pen [a pen that you dip into ink]—the Deleter pens are my favorite.

What are great ways for kids to create comics right now?
All you need to make a comic is a piece of paper and a pencil. After you draw a comic, it's really easy to distribute it. One option is to put it online— post it on a personal blog, share it on Facebook, or join an art-sharing site

like deviantART. You can also make photocopies if you have access to a [copy] machine. Just copy, staple, and give them to your friends!

The Secret Science Alliance and the Copycat Crook © Eleanor Davis

How do you use technology to create comics?

I have a Wacom tablet, which I do a lot of sketching on, but I do my final art in pencil on paper and then ink it with real ink. The coloring I usually do on the computer, using Photoshop. I also post comics to my website and blog.

The Secret Science Alliance and the Copycat Crook © Eleanor Davis

Why is telling a story with comics important to you?

I love telling stories, and I love drawing. I've been reading and writing comics for so long, I even think in comics. I don't have a better way of explaining it than that!

How do you use social media to create or promote your work?

I'm not the best at social media, but I do post about my work on Twitter and Facebook. I love it! It's great to get encouragement and feedback—making art can often be very solitary, but now with the Internet it doesn't need to be.

Pencils: Okay . . . everybody knows about pencils, but not all pencils are good for drawing. A standard No. 2 pencil will work for penciling your comics, but you might want to try professional art pencils as well.

Art pencils come in different degrees of hard and soft leads, so test them out and see what you like. An H on the pencil means the lead is hard, so the pencil will produce a tight, light line and will give you greater detail. A B on a pencil means that the lead is soft, so the pencil will produce a darker line and will create better shading effects. The higher the number on the pencil, the softer or harder the lead (8B is really soft; 6H is really hard). An HB means it has a good balance of both—*Comics in Your Curriculum* author Richard Jenkins digs the HB.

Colored pencils: If you'd like to produce color comics for fun, a set of twelve or twenty-four soft, lead-centered colored pencils is wonderful to have. Colored pencils are easier to control and use than paint or colored inks. Prismacolor makes several different sets, but shop around and see what suits your needs best.

Blue pencils: Lots of professional comics artists use light-blue pencils to first sketch out their drawings. They then ink over them with a brush, Pigma pen, or crow quill. The blue pencil helps provide a good guide for the ink and won't show up when you make copies of your inked pages on a copy machine.

Brushes: An excellent brush for inking is the Winsor & Newton Series 7, size 3, for use with black India ink. But again, try different ones and see what you like. Ideally, look for a round, sable-head brush. A round-head brush gives you more versatility than a flathead brush. Sable brushes hold ink well and won't splay after repeated cleaning and use. They range in size from 9, the largest, to 000, the smallest. The

Comics creators can get pretty special awards. Art Spiegelman's *Maus* is the only comic to earn a Pulitzer Prize. David Mazzucchelli's *Asterios Polyp* won the first *Los Angeles Times* Book Prize for a comic. Gene Yang's *American Born Chinese* was the first comic to be nominated for a National Book Award.

Winsor & Newton Series 7 is an excellent brush, but expensive. Check out chapter 11 at the back of this book for more art-supply websites.

Crow quills: A crow quill is a versatile tool that you can use when inking your comics. Crow quills are like calligraphy pens: you dip them in ink, like a brush. They have a rigid head and combine the stiffness of a pen with the varied line weight you get from a brush.

India ink: Brushes and crow quills both use India ink. It's not a brand name; it's the blackest ink you can get. Typically, comics are inked with India ink, but feel free to experiment with other colors. India ink is permanent and waterproof, although you should still avoid getting your pages wet. Even though you can't erase India ink, you can use correction liquid to cover any mistakes. The ink takes at least two or three minutes to dry (watch out for smudges in the meantime!). Some good brands to keep an eye out for are Pelikan and Higgins Black Magic. India ink usually comes in a glass or plastic jar, which you can dip your brush right in.

Charcoal sticks: Charcoal sticks can be messy and may take some getting used to, but once you master them, they produce a line that seems to breathe a bit more than ink (although most comics pages are inked). Charcoal is fantastic for sketching and working out your ideas on paper. Try a Ritmo charcoal pencil from Italy—it's less messy than a typical charcoal stick and gives you greater range.

Magic Markers: If you're not ready for India ink just yet, you can also use a Magic Marker to ink over your penciled illustrations. Magic Markers don't give you as varied a line as a brush, but they're fun and a great complementary tool to master.

Brush pens: Brush pens have ink in them like a marker, but a flexible head like a brush to give you varied line weight. Sakura and Pentel both make really nice brush pens that come in several different sizes and colors.

RULERS

Rulers can be helpful for drawing panels and laying out your comic. A standard twelve-inch ruler should work well for any measurements you'll need to make. Eighteen-inch metal rulers with cork underneath are helpful because they're slightly flexible and won't slip. T-squares are good, too, but more expensive. As an exercise, try to draw straight lines without one, when you can. The old-school artists can freehand straight lines over and over.

CORRECTION FLUID

Inking your comics can be tricky, so you might want to use some white correction liquid for any corrections you may need to make when you ink. Use it with a small brush, as if it were regular ink, and carefully dab it wherever needed. Some artists expand beyond just using it for corrections, creating added contrast and texture along with India ink.

Did you notice I didn't put *eraser* on the list? I suggest not using one, especially when sketching. At this stage, there are no mistakes! You're still learning, so don't erase anything, even if you think a drawing doesn't look right. It's much better to draw that same thing again. You'll be surprised how fast you improve if you avoid using erasers while drawing. Later, compare early sketches to new ones to see how you've grown.

Your tools and studio are about individual style and preference, and everyone's style and inspiration is totally different. Every artist has his or her own choice of paper, pens, pencils, and brushes. Certain artists swear by certain tools. Others use just about anything under the sun, depending on the effect they're trying to achieve. How you use these tools to perfect your illustration technique will reflect your own personal flair and comic book style.

Soon you'll be using the same kinds of pens, pencils, brushes, and paper that your favorite artists use to create comics masterpieces. But don't worry about dropping a lot of money on these items. Right now, you can use the pencils, markers, and pens that you already have lying around the house. The most important thing is to draw as much as possible, and let your imagination guide you to new opportunities.

EDWARD SULLIVAN

Age: 15
Education: Tenth-grade student
His Comic: Big Bot

What are your favorite comic books?
I enjoy *Star Wars* comics, mostly because of the designs of the characters and because I have always enjoyed *Star Wars* lore. I also enjoy a variety of DC/Marvel comics. If I had to pinpoint one type, it would be *Green Lantern* comics. I always like the character variation and the constructs. Recently, a friend introduced me to a limited series [the total number of issues that will be created is set before production in a limited series], *Atomic Robo*. It is a funny series, and the main robot's design is cool.

Why do you like creating comics?
I like creating new stories. I especially like making new characters, usually with a lot of gadgets.

Where do you get the inspiration for your creations?
Some inspiration comes from *Star Wars* or the *Halo* video game, but also some comes from DC and Marvel superhero comics.

What are your favorite tools to use when writing and drawing comics?
Mainly just paper and pencil.

Does technology help you create?
I don't really make anything with computers, but if there is a pose that is difficult to draw or inspiration I cannot get my hands on, there are many online comics.

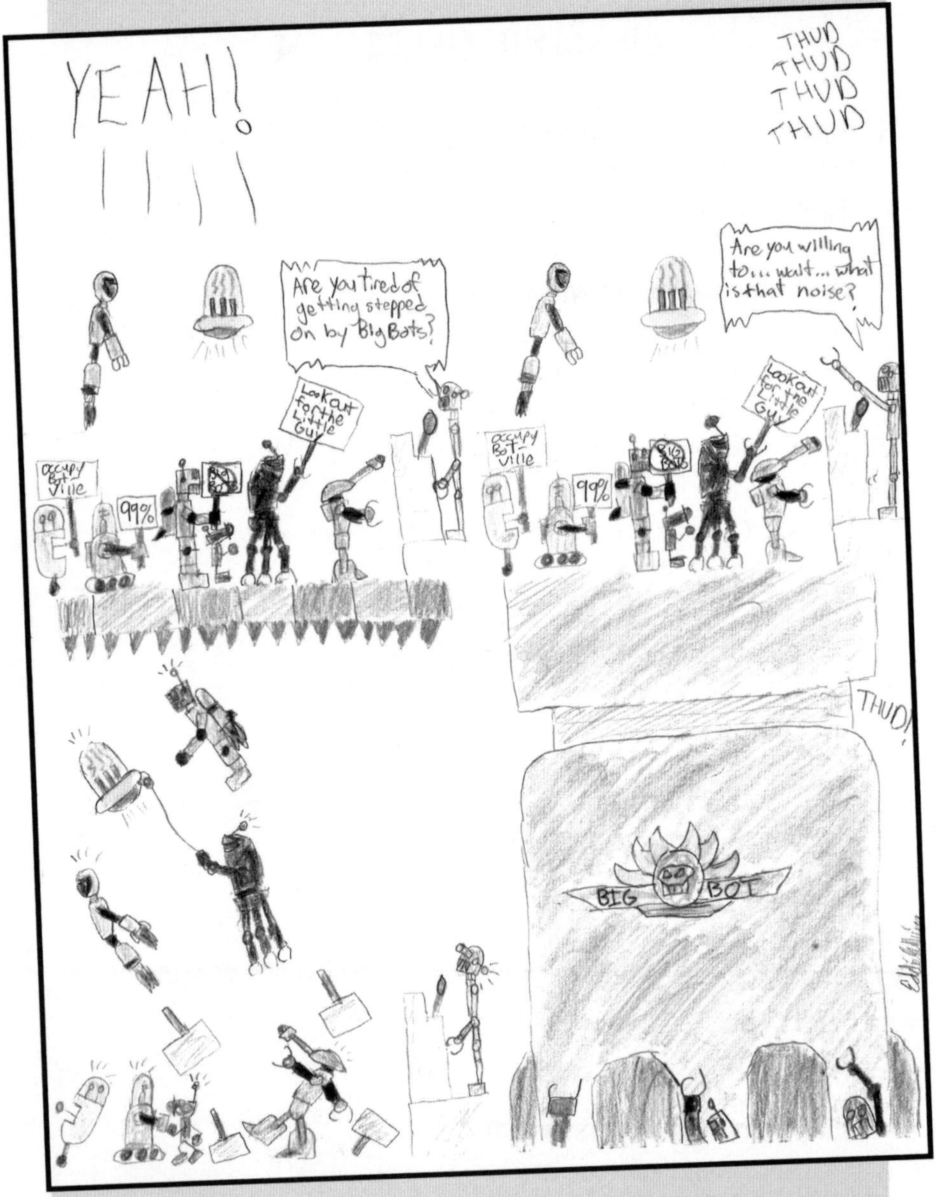
YEAH!
THUD
THUD
THUD
THUD
Are you tired of getting stepped on by Big Bots?
Occupy Bot-ville
99%
Look out for the Little Guys
Big Bots
Are you willing to... wait... what is that noise?
THUD!
BIG BOT

How do you think making comics could help you in other creative careers?

Comics can help with graphic design, video game character design, or movie animation.

What are your plans for the future?

Video game concept art/design has always interested me. That could be a cool job.

What's the best advice you can give your peers?

When you have an idea, stick with it and try to evolve it until you feel it is your best work and you are genuinely excited to work with it. Usually, when I am really into a character, I can add things and develop him to the point where I wish I could jump into his shoes.

31

DRAW, PARTNER!
ILLUSTRATION TIPS AND
TRICKS

For some of you, drawing your comic may sound challenging, but with a little practice and a few tips, you can create awesome illustrations. Now that you have your studio set up and own a few tools, the next step is to get your ideas down on paper.

DOODLE MOOD

As far as your ideas go, you're not going to remember every brainstorm you have. *Write them down.* If you come up with an outstanding new character—a superhero, a zombie, a robot from the twenty-third century—make a doodle, or quick drawing of it. It's okay if your idea changes later on.

Ignore anyone who tells you, "That's a weird idea." Some friends and I came up with an idea for a talking gorilla called Sky Ape that flew around with a jetpack. People thought we were crazy. "A talking gorilla?!" they said. But, we ended up doing a four-issue Sky Ape series, a book-length collection, and then more books, called *Waiting for Crime*, *All the Heroes*, and *King of Girls*, with that character. *Entertainment Weekly* magazine announced that it was the second-best idea in the history of comics! Imagine if my pals and I had been too shy to even try?

The best way to keep track of your ideas and doodles is with a journal. An idea journal is your creative playground for brainstorming new ideas and sketches. Back to front, upside down, vertical, or horizontal—how you use it doesn't matter. It can help you flesh out your stories and characters. When you need a jolt of creativity, your journal can act as a file cabinet for your best ideas. Got an idea for a dentist who helps vampires with tooth—er, fang—aches? Make a few doodles in your idea journal of what the vampires look like. Then change them, and change them again, until you get the vibe you like. Jot down some notes on what the first story might be about and where it takes place.

Put your notes and your doodles on the same page, and don't move on to the next page until the first is filled up. An idea journal is not necessarily about being neat or orderly—it's about going where your imagination takes you. Keep the drawings you create. You never know when you might need to look back and find some extra inspiration. (I still have stories and comics scripts on my laptop that I might never get around to publishing, but I love going back and getting inspiration from them.)

SKETCH STRETCH!

Sketching is something you can do right now to improve your skills as an artist. The very first comics you ever draw are going to look rough—they're *supposed* to look that way, so don't get discouraged. Every comic book artist begins with sketches.

What's the difference between doodles and sketches? For me, doodles are daydreamy drawings that get the inspiration out of my head and onto paper—or a napkin, or a birthday card, and so on—as soon as the idea hits me. Sketching is about working out my style. Think of it like stretching your muscles before jogging or playing in a game. The more you stretch, the more flexible you are, and the better you'll play. Sketching is also about noticing subject matter. If you're sketching your cat sleeping on a cushy chair, notice how it curls its body and positions its paws, or how the sun from the window creates light and shadow on its face.

Try to sketch as often as possible. Remember, established comics artists have spent years perfecting their drawing techniques, whether they went to art school or not. No matter what age they started creating comics, they all drew hundreds of sketches before they even thought of being published. They sketched tons of things from real life *and* things from their imagination. That's what you're going to do, too.

COMIC BOOK WORKOUT

Giving characters expressions and body language will help tell your tale even before words sparkle on the page. When you're starting out, though, that's easier said than done. How do you shake the stiffness from your pencil and still have your story reflect who you are? Breathe life into those stick fingers! Try some of these exercises to help limber you up.

> **The Word Wall:** I use this one with my students all the time. We pick a category and think of words from A to Z that fit the category. So, think of character traits—likeable, bossy, calm, and so forth. Write the words on index cards, then pin or tape them to your wall or a board (foam core or science-project trifolds work great). Then draw an expression, gesture, or body pose to go with each one. Now you have handy reference sketches for your comics that cover a wide range of emotions.

Call to Action: Pick an average situation—making your bed, grocery shopping, mowing the lawn—and give it high-octane punch! Once you've sketched your characters from head to toe, draw them again, this time from several different angles—side views, top views, action shots, from behind, you name it. Keep these sketches as a guide for creating future illustrations. Will Eisner could draw characters floating into rooms and cars bucking off the road. If he wanted, Eisner could have made a comic about sewing that buzzed with boxing-ring energy. Another comics legend, Wally Wood, is famous for his "22 Panels That Always Work," which can be easily found online.

The Replacements: Choose one of your favorite three-panel comic strips from the newspaper or online. On a piece of sketch paper, draw the strip. Don't trace, and don't worry about copying the artist's style to perfection. Next, draw a second strip, this time replacing the comic strip characters with your own. Study what's different and what's the same. Learn from their compositions and style: how facial expressions and body language project emotion, or how simple gestures can say more than words sometimes.

COMICS CREATOR

SAM HENDERSON

From: Woodstock, New York
Job: Cartoonist
His Comics: *The Magic Whistle*; a feature called "Scene But Not Heard" for *Nickelodeon Magazine*; *SpongeBob SquarePants* (writer, 2001)

"Scene But Not Heard" (from *Nickelodeon Magazine*) © Sam Henderson

What was your first or favorite comic when you were younger?

I was into *MAD* and if a new one wasn't out, I'd get one if its competitors. My mother worked for the local paper, so I'd see all the funnies through that. Like most eventual cartoonists, I especially liked *Peanuts*. My father saved all sorts of things most people throw away. As a result, I saw all the comics he collected in the fifties like ECs [EC Comics] before they were reprinted multiple times. From kindergarten to twelfth grade, I'd rush home to see animation [on television] from the major Hollywood studios.

When did you know you wanted to make comics?

After seeing the [Hollywood shows], I decided that's what I wanted to do. I assumed everything I saw was known in every household and anybody who did a comic was famous.

What kinds of things inspire your comic book creations?

Life around me. Like when I see my fan out of the corner of my eye, I think of situations that would involve fans. Right now I'm working on a longer comic about my childhood and spending enough time in my hometown to remember specific locations [I first knew] more than thirty years ago.

What tools do you use to create your comics?

Mostly Micron [pens], which are kind of a combination of felt-tips and rapidographs. You don't have to clean them like rapidographs, and they don't bleed or change point sizes like markers.

What are great ways for kids to create comics right now?

Keep a sketchbook with you, so when you come up with an idea, you can execute it. The final comic is a more legible version of what you've done before. Computers are good now to scan the work and make files.

How do you use technology to create comics?

In high school and college, I used to make a Xerox comic and mail it to thirty to fifty people; now you can put it on the Internet and get feedback right away without having to buy stamps or go to the post office. You can also instantly fix it if necessary. If you're messy like I am, you can Photoshop it to clean up any smudges or erasures and forget ever having to do color on paper unless you want to.

Why is telling a story with comics important to you?

For me, it's easier to communicate an idea using words and pictures without having to use either of those methods alone. It's also something to do without needing people to cooperate exactly the way you want them to.

How did making comics prepare you for writing for *SpongeBob SquarePants*?

It was from seeing my comics that they decided they wanted to use my sense of humor and aesthetics.

How do you use social media to create or promote your work?

Facebook is good for publicity and getting feedback, so you'll know what people think. There have been times when I've redrawn something because of what somebody suggested, and it turned out to be a better solution. It's easier to promote or show what you're working on without having to pay money or wait until you can get together with somebody.

Life, Less Ordinary: Focusing on just faces this time, exaggerate and distort different features. What would your character look like with a bulbous forehead and chubby cheeks? How about a long nose and crooked teeth? Or pull a "Dr. Jekyll and Mr. Hyde" and morph your character over three poses, from respectable to unruly to downright monstrous! You don't need to be realistic all the time. In fact, comics characters can have exaggerated, even outlandish, features. The eyes and mouths are especially expressive. You can also interchange facial features Mr. Potato Head–style to create an almost limitless variety of expressions for one face. From *Billy Batson and the Magic of Shazam!*'s Mike Kunkel all the way back to Basil Wolverton and Will Elder, artists are ready to give their characters every emotion under the sun.

Buzz Word: Warm up your creative juices by transforming someone else's words into images. Think of one of your favorite books or songs, and draw how you envision the setting and characters. Or randomly pick three words from the dictionary (*pineapple, automobile, flabby*), and see if that inspires an original character and story.

Switcheroo: Sketches and doodles don't have to be with a pencil. Try drawing the same objects with different items: pens, charcoal, markers, paints. Notice the variety of results. You can also make up a tool of your own (like Q-tips or toothbrushes). When you master a unique tool, it can be your secret weapon for making a good comic.

Shape-shifter: Choose five objects of different shapes and sizes from around your house. Keep the shapes simple. Draw your five objects quickly with a pencil, and then try to transform the objects into interesting characters. A balloon shape can meld into Jigglypuff from *Pokémon*. A few cones and cylinders might morph into *Star Wars* droids. Circles, ovals, squares, and triangles will transform into cute or scary characters before you know it. You might never look at your living room lamp the same way again.

INKING YOUR SKETCHES

Typically, comic book artists use a pencil to rough out the drawings and then a pen or brush to ink over the pencil. When you're done trying these sketching exercises, try inking over your work with a felt-tip pen or marker for practice before you try brushes or crow quills. You can even ink on tracing paper, so your pencil drawings underneath remain untouched, and you can practice inking over them as many times as you want. Don't worry about making your illustrations perfect—think about comics as a process.

YOU NEVER KNOW WHAT HEROES, ALIENS, OR SUSHI CHEFS LURK IN THOSE "LOLLIPOP" DOODLES.

1. Doodle up that sketchbook page with a light pencil. Try drawing basic shapes. Circles, ovals, and squiggles can be pretty expressive.

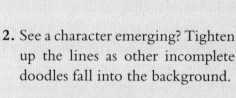

2. See a character emerging? Tighten up the lines as other incomplete doodles fall into the background.

3. Add details. Refine the lines.

4. Color or shade for weight and depth. Boys and girls, I give you METRO, master of time and space, and our only hope against the dreaded pizza virus!

ART SCHOOL?

You don't have to go to art school to be a comics artist. Many comics artists are self-taught. But keep in mind, if you don't go to art school, you need to be the kind of person who really understands commitment. You must hold yourself accountable to achieve a dream, because you know the rewards are worth it.

Cow & Buffalo creator Mike Maihack went to Columbus College of Art & Design. Fan favorite Humberto Ramos is self-taught. Pop Mhan studied formal technical drawing but is self-taught when it comes to comics. Alex Maleev spent some time at The Kubert School and then ventured out on his own.

There are excellent art schools at the high school level (like The Center School in Seattle and the Artists for Humanity program in Boston) and at the college level (tons in chapter 11: Resources) all over the country. Some offer programs that focus specifically on drawing comics. Art school, in general, teaches you things such as anatomy, perspective, composition, media, color theory, storytelling, and even sculpture. Some specialize in doing all of that art and design on computer. There's no right answer to whether or not to go to art school for comics. Take some time to think about it. The good thing is, nothing's stopping you from creating comics right *now*.

AN ORIGINAL COMIC

Your journal is going to become very valuable to you, as a budding comics creator. It's a diary of your work. It's the place to create whatever springs into your mind, no matter how strange, wacky, or unique the idea may be. Chances are, you'll come up with a truly original comic based on these early concepts, doodles, and sketches, so don't second-guess your creativity and dedication. Those are the things that will make your comic book stand out in the crowd.

YOUNG COMICS CREATOR

JUSTIN LEE

Age: 14
Education: Ninth-grade student
His Comic: *Armortek*

What are your favorite comic books?

My favorite comics are *Naruto* and *Akira*. Also superhero comics like *Superman* and *Spider-Man*. I like these comics because they have good stories, action, and artwork.

Why do you like creating comics?

I love creating comics because it's fun. I love to design characters, create stories, and I just love to draw.

Where do you get the inspiration for your creations?

I get my inspirations from my dad. (He's a professional in the animation business.) I love his drawings and how he tells his stories. He introduced me to comics and animation, where I also get my inspiration.

What are your favorite tools to use when writing and drawing comics?

My favorite tools are pencil and eraser, and pen.

Does technology help you create?

No, just pencil, eraser, and pen.

How do you think making comics could help you in other careers?
It could help me become a professional comic book artist, an animator, a director, or other jobs in the film business. Making comics helps me improve on storytelling, and it is a skill you need to achieve to be a filmmaker.

What are your plans for the future?

I plan to improve on my storytelling and drawing skills and then I'll self-publish my book. Hopefully, a major publisher will be interested in my book, and they would publish my book to reach a wider audience.

What's the best advice you can give your peers?

My advice is to keep up the practice of drawing every day, drawing from life. Be inspired by your favorite artists, studying their techniques and understanding the concepts. Learning from the "how to" drawing books can really get you started.

CHARACTER CREATION: FROM SUPERHEROES TO VILLAINS

You rise from the old city reservoir, covered in radioactive muck. Once, you were human, but now you are superstrong and nearly invincible. Unfortunately, the poisonous goo also made you a freakish creature that terrifies everyone who crosses your path. Oh, wait ... it's not you! It's your comic book character!

Comic book characters come in all shapes and sizes, from superheroes to monsters to ordinary kids doing extraordinary things. What kinds of characters do you envision for your comic book? How about a tragic mutant like *X-Men*'s Wolverine, or a goofball like *Archie*'s Jughead who bumbles into mischief? Your characters can personify a concept using the elements of fire, water, earth, and sky. Maybe your comic is about you. In that case, you and your friends can become the characters.

How you choose your character comes from the kinds of comics you enjoy. Do you play *World of Warcraft* online? If so, you might develop a character based on your game avatar, like a magus or a warrior. If you are fascinated with Japanese anime, you could model your character after Toriko the gourmet hunter, or Monkey D. Luffy the treasure hunter in *One Piece*. That doesn't mean swipe someone's character and just change the hat and shoes, but use inspiration from other characters to feed your brain and ideas.

COMING UP WITH A CHARACTER

There isn't one perfect set of rules for creating characters, but there are some guidelines that can help you lay the foundation of your character's personality, history, and motivation. Once you know these basics, all that's left to do is choose which of your characters to draw first!

Famous Funnies is widely regarded as being the first comic book in the size and shape that we know it today. In the 1930s, it sold for only ten cents!

ORIGIN: THE BOY FROM KRYPTON

As you create your character, imagine an origin for him or her. Basically, origin is the place your characters come from and how they got to be where they are now. Probably everybody knows the story of Superman's origin. Before the planet Krypton explodes, a scientist named Jor-El spares his baby son, Kal-El, by placing him safely in a rocket pod and sending him millions of miles through space to Earth, where the energy from our sun gives him the powers of Superman. His only weakness?

48

Kryptonite—a harmless substance for us earthlings, this abundant mineral on Superman's home planet blocks his superpowers on Earth.

For your characters, try writing down a few sentences about their origins. It doesn't have to be fancy. Where did they come from? How did they get here? Who saw them first? And how does that background relate to events that happen in the present and future?

MOTIVATION: BEHIND THE MASK OF THE CAPED CRUSADER

Character motivation can explain why a character acts or reacts a certain way and is an important part of your character's personality. Bruce Wayne's parents are attacked and killed by a mugger when he's just a boy. In the role of Batman, the orphaned millionaire vows to protect the innocent people of Gotham City from similar fates. Batman's motivation for fighting crime is his parents' death. Sometimes, similar events can create different motivations for different characters. Within the same world, Oswald Cobblepot is also an orphan. But while Bruce Wayne becomes the heroic Batman, Oswald Cobblepot chooses a life of crime as the despicable villain, the Penguin.

PERSONALITY: THE GOOD, THE BAD, AND THE SURPRISINGLY BEWILDERED?

You might want to give your characters more dynamic personality traits than the "good guys" versus the "bad guys." If you limit your characters to these common traits, you may find that your comics become flat and unexciting. Try to keep your readers on their toes! Character personality is what you'll articulate in the pages of your comic with your character's expressions, actions, and dialogue. For example, the X-Men all have very different personalities. It makes them an interesting group.

Cyclops: Dull but brave, a consummate leader

Colossus: Noble and selfless in the face of danger

Wolverine: Unflinching in battle, a bit volatile

Storm: Reserved but with emotions always bubbling just beneath the surface

Choose strong adjectives! Create characters with clear descriptors: excitable, aloof, sneaky, spoiled, scared, forgetful, lively, glum, fortunate, impolite, daring, charismatic, grateful, graceful, ambitious, witty, pompous, and punctilious. (That last one means they pay attention to details.)

The most interesting heroes and champions have faults. Look at Marvel Comics' Spider-Man, Iron Man, Thor, Hulk, Daredevil, and Fantastic Four—all have some kind of imperfection, and readers have followed their stories for decades. In a more recent example, the main character of Jonathan Case's graphic novel *Dear Creature* is a love-starved sea mutant with a taste for Shakespeare ... and human flesh.

Just the name of a character can become an important story element. Characters' names may be descriptive of their personalities, both with heroes and villains. Sometimes the names become another element of the story. For example, in the classic Asterix series, French creators René Goscinny and Albert Uderzo chose to make all the rebellious Gauls' names end in "ix," and all of them are a play on words, usually descriptive of the characters' personalities: Getafix the druid, Cacofonix the bard; the names of the Roman invaders (the bad guys) all end in "us," such as Brutus and Cantankerus.

As a character exercise, practice observing the personalities of people around you: your friends, family, and people at school or on the street. Use these personalities as models for your own characters. Pay attention to the qualities that make people unique. The pros do it all the time. You can bet there's a superhero out there based on someone's favorite uncle, a villain based on an iron-fisted school librarian, or a love interest based on a high school crush.

Heroes Versus Villains

Heroes and villains are two of the most common character types found in comic books. Captain America was frozen during World War II and then unfrozen later to protect the innocent from evil. The Red Skull is a dangerous foe with plans to dominate the entire world. The former is a hero, and the latter is a villain. A classic hero is typically motivated to defend the less fortunate, uphold justice, show compassion, and foster hope. A classic villain can be self-serving, hateful, and manipulative. Your character doesn't have to fall into a "classic" hero or villain category—these are just examples.

It's great if your heroes win most of their battles, but they don't have to excel at every turn. Some failures will improve your characters' believability and make for a more exciting adventure. To mix this classic structure up a bit, some creators like to play with the roles even more by developing an anti-hero, a "good guy" who should behave well but is conspicuously lacking in heroic qualities, or a "bad guy" who retains some roguish appeal, despite despicable actions. Marvel's Wolverine from the X-Men doesn't exactly behave like a Boy Scout now, does he? The Punisher seems so thirsty for revenge it's put him at odds with his fellow heroes, like Daredevil.

Comics influence popular culture, weaving their way into song titles and lyrics, like "Magneto and Titanium Man" by Paul McCartney and Wings and "Superman" by The Kinks. Creators get props, too. The Beastie Boys cite counterculture comic and animation artist Vaughn Bode as an influence, and Pop Will Eat Itself sing, "Alan Moore [*Watchmen, V for Vendetta*] knows the score!"

MIKE MAIHACK

From: Tampa, Florida
Job: Graphic designer, comic artist
His Comics: *Cleopatra in Space, Cow & Buffalo, Comic Book Tattoo* (contributor), Jim Henson's *The Storyteller* (contributor)

What was your first or favorite comic when you were younger?

The *X-Men*. I loved the team dynamic, the long history of the characters and how most of them were just teenagers trying to fit in. I mean, fighting for their lives to fit in, but trying to fit in nonetheless.

When did you know you wanted to make comics?

Since I was around five, when my mom gave me the Sunday funnies, some paper, and some crayons. It wasn't till I read Jeff Smith's *Bone* that I thought about drawing actual comic *books*, though. As much as I loved reading them, I had no desire to draw superhero comics. Later I realized I just didn't want to spend my time writing someone else's characters. I wanted to make up and tell my own stories.

What kinds of things inspire your comic book creations?

Movies, music, comic books, cartoons, taking a walk in the park, a really tasty burrito, my cats . . . everything really! Some stuff influences certain stories more than others. For instance, pulp sci-fi and spaghetti Westerns, as well as movies like *Star Wars* and *Star Trek*, are huge influences on *Cleopatra in Space*. But there are a lot of aspects from my surroundings that I bring, even subconsciously, into my characters.

What tools do you use to create your comics?

Everything I draw is first penciled with the same refillable Koh-I-Noor Rapidomatic Pencil I've had since college. You can find them at any art store. I use a blue lead since I like the softer feel. I ink traditionally as well, with a

Cleopatra in Space © Mike Maihack

size 02 Sakura Micron—although lately that inking has become more of a forty-sixty split of both traditional and digital. And almost all my coloring and lettering is done digitally in Photoshop.

Cleopatra in Space © Mike Maihack

What are great ways for kids to create comics right now?

I'd say first by taking a look at the comics you enjoy and thinking a little about what it is you enjoy about them. Then it's just about finding something to draw with and something to draw on. Maybe start by trying to depict something that happened to you today. At home, at school, on the bus. Challenge yourself into telling a story in three to six panels. Or make up a character or two, and start telling one-page comics about their adventures. As you grow more comfortable with those single-page strips, start moving on to longer stories. Most of all, don't get caught up thinking there are any right or wrong ways to making a comic, because there aren't. Simply tell a story, draw it in pictures, and place it in a sequence.

How do you use technology to create comics?

I use a computer, primarily Photoshop, to color most of my comics. Also the panel borders, lettering, and various tweaks here and there are done digitally. And since many of my comics go on the Internet, I rely on technology to present my comics to the world.

Why is telling a story with comics important to you?

I'm a visual storyteller. Whether it be by comics or animation, I like to see what the story is about. I respond more to the combination of words and pictures—even more so when those pictures are cartoons. Unlike animation, however, comics are something I'm able to create all by myself. There's no team needed, just me, so I'm afforded the ability to tell any story I want. I'm a huge fan of dialogue as well, and telling a story through comics allows me to tell a story with minimal exposition.

How do you use social media to create or promote your work?

Anytime I draw new comics, I use all the various social media to let others know it's up on the web or out in stores. Since that is the way most people follow creators nowadays, it's become almost essential to be part of the social network in order for people to be aware of your work. Simply posting a comic or information to one site and hoping a readership will follow isn't enough. More importantly, I've made a lot of friends through these networks. Since making comics can at times be a pretty isolated career, having the ability to chat with friends at your fingertips is wonderful!

Personality Profile

Ask yourself these starter questions to help determine your character's personality profile.

Personal-narrative profile (for nonfiction comics):
- Where was your character born?
- What is your character's family like?
- What big events and small events make your character who he is today?

Superhero profile (for fiction comics):
- What kind of superpower does your character have?
- How did your character get her amazing powers?
- Does your character have a secret identity?

Action hero profile (for adventure comics):
- Does your character have a costume that hides his identity?
- Are there any special tools, powers, or equipment that your character uses?
- Does your character have cool transportation (like Batman's Batmobile or Wonder Woman's invisible plane)?

Wizard profile (for fantasy comics):
- When and how did your magic character discover her powers?
- What spells is he trying to master?
- Does your wizard have any gear (magic wand, amulet) or a familiar (an owl, a dragon) to assist her on a quest?

Character Creations

Here are some ideas to get you started on your own character creations.

Star Power: When creating your comic book characters, you can always use your own life as inspiration. You could do a *great* comic book simply about your triumphs and challenges. Take one of your experiences and panel it out in comics format. Ever wished you could change your past, or tell your point of view on something that happened? This time, the outcome is all in your hands.

Family Matters: Try creating characters out of your family members and closest friends. If your grandma had a superpower, what would it be? Maybe your mom actually *does* have eyes in the back of her head. Think about others' strongest traits, good and bad, and have fun mixing their personalities.

Alter Ego: Think about a famous comic character who seems to have another side to him. Mild Bruce Banner transforms into the invincible Hulk. Dr. Donald Blake walks with a cane before he becomes the Norse god, Thor. Clark Kent pretends to be a klutz when he's not Superman. Use this idea of the alter ego to create your own interesting characters from ones you already know. For example, a shy student could secretly be the superhero who just saved the planet from a destructive asteroid.

Planet Animal: Create a story where all the characters are animals. Each animal can represent a different character personality in your story. A nasty bulldog can be the track coach, or a pesky chicken can be a nosy neighbor. What

Sometimes comics characters get makeovers. Originally, the Hulk was gray, not green. Even whole universes can get renovated, like with DC Comics' *Infinite Crisis* and *Flashpoint*, and Marvel's *The Infinity Gauntlet* and *Marvel Knights*.

animals could you use to create a character who is brave, sinister, honest, or curious? What character traits would you give to pigeons, crows, squirrels, and ducks if they could interact the way people do?

BE INSPIRED!

Your hero is a brave champion from a far planet. His nemesis is a villainous creature, thawed after centuries in Arctic ice. Their battles will become the stuff of legends, and you're the one who gets to create their adventures! In comics, you can build any kind of characters you want and put them into any kind of story. You can create superheroes, be inspired by manga, invent some wacky animal characters, or create stories about ordinary people. The trick is to add something of yourself, on some level, to all your creations. Use your experience and instincts to give them that extra punch. It'll help set your comics apart from everything else.

In 1961, Marvel Comics tried something different with the creation of the Fantastic Four, a superhero family that didn't wear masks and made no attempt to hide their identities.

EVAN OKUI

Age: 8
Education: Third-grade student
His Comic: Silver Shadow

In Texas, there was a superhero named Silver Shadow. He could fight.

Hi!

At the bank of Texas, there was a robbery. A guy was stealing money

Heh Heh Heh

Bank of Texas

Then, Silver Shadow saw the guy and chased him when he saw him.

Charge

So Silver Shadow got closer and closer until he was behind him.

Ya

Ah

What are your favorite comic books?

My favorite comics are LEGO comics because there's a lot of action. I like the *Star Wars*, *Pirates of the Caribbean*, and *Ninjago* stories.

Why do you like creating comics?

I like creating comics because it's fun, and I get to create my own characters. I'm happy I can write whatever I want.

Where do you get the inspirations for your creations?

I get my ideas from books such as *Captain Underpants*. I also get ideas from TV shows. Or sometimes I just think of ideas on my own.

What are your favorite tools to use when writing and drawing comics?

My favorite tools to use for writing and drawing are pencils, colored pencils, and crayons. I make my comic books by stapling paper together, so it looks like a real book. I like to use colored staples, so when I color the page, it's hard to see the staples.

Does technology help you create?

I also use comics templates that my mom created on Adobe Illustrator for me.

What are your plans for the future?

I would like to have them published and sold in bookstores.

What's the best advice you can give your peers?

Get your ideas from things you like, and try your best. Make your comic to be whatever you want it to be about. Sometimes I plan the stories before I start drawing them. Those ones turn out the best.

CREATING STELLAR STORIES: COMIC BOOK SCRIPTS

Now that you've started writing and sketching your character ideas in your sketchpad and idea journal, the next step is creating the world they inhabit . . . and, of course, deciding what they do there! This chapter is all about how to create action-packed stories for your comic.

PICK A GENRE . . . ANY GENRE

There are tons of comics out there with as many different story styles as there are readers. There are superhero comics like *Superman*, *Iron Man*, *Batman*, and *Spider-Man*. There are non-superhero comics, too, from classics like *The Adventures of Tintin* and *Maison Ikkoku* to cool newer stuff like *Bastion's 7*, *ChocoMimi*, and *Glister*. Whatever your tastes might be, turn to your favorite things for inspiration. Seemingly unrelated interests can lead to fascinatingly fresh ideas.

Jonathan Case combined a love for Shakespeare's poetry, B horror movies from the fifties, and classic comics from the thirties and forties to create *Dear Creature*. Mixing genres can also have interesting effects. Mirage Studios' *Teenage Mutant Ninja Turtles* series combines traditional samurai martial arts with gritty modern crime fighting.

There are so many exciting genres in comics: science fiction, horror, Westerns, martial arts, superheroes, real-life adventure ... The list goes on. Think of your favorite movie and then try to figure out what genre that movie belongs to. *X-Men* would be the superhero genre. *Star Wars* would be science fiction. *Harry Potter* would be sword-and-sorcery, or fantasy. Use that genre to inspire your comics story. Ask your teachers to help you learn more about specific genres like biographies, memoirs, poetry, science fiction, fables, folk tales, realistic fiction ...

WRITING THE PERFECT COMIC BOOK STORY

Now that you've determined what genre you would like to try, you're ready to put together a comic book story. Here are some helpful questions to ask yourself when devising the perfect tale.

Characters: Who's in your comic? A superhero family? A talking dog? You?

Plot: What will your characters do? Compete in a galactic race? Look for a new home?

Setting: Where do your characters live? In what time period? Yesterday? The future?

Goal: What do your characters want? Does one want to be the greatest knight in the land?

Rising action: What's happening as the characters shoot for that goal? Who's trying to stop them?

Climax: How will the hero and the villain have their ultimate, face-to-face battle?

Outcome: Did your characters reach their goals? Is the setting a better place now?

PREMISE

Most comic book stories start with a premise or idea. *Spider-Man*'s premise is that teenager Peter Parker is bitten by a radio-active spider, and he becomes a superhuman crime fighter. Peter Parker might not talk about that premise in every issue, but it's the one event that changes everything in his life after it. What will be your story's premise?

Caped, cowled superheroes are almost nonexistent in Japanese manga. But you'll find basketball (*Slam Dunk*), baseball, (*Dokaben*), and even animals, like the cat in *Chi's Sweet Home* and the frog in *Keroro Gunso*.

THEME

Themes are often big abstract concepts that readers understand from reading the story, but they aren't always stated explicitly. Good versus evil may be one of the most common themes across all genres, and particularly in stories with epic proportions. Other main themes or supporting themes might be revenge, impossible love, prejudice, acceptance, breaking roles or stereotypes, or showing the importance of a small detail from ordinary life.

A theme doesn't need to be complex—it's any subject or topic of discussion that concerns you. After all, if you're driven to create a comic, you surely have something to say about the world around you. This can be your comic book theme. If you can't think of a theme, don't worry: sometimes as you write a story, the theme emerges as the plot and characters develop.

You might be surprised by some of the themes found in your favorite comics. *X-Men* comics have dealt with social topics. *Spider-Man* reminds us that with greater power comes greater responsibility. My own comic, *The Nevermen*—with moody art by Guy Davis—has some heavy ideas about what makes a hero, but it's wrapped up in lots of bare-knuckle action. Can you make a list of ten issues or topics that affect you in your life? Do you feel safe in the town where you live? Are there bullies at school? Is there litter floating in the river where you used to fish? Is there something on the news that concerns you? Now, try turning that issue into a theme for your story.

PLOT

The series of events that make up your story is called the plot. Your comics journal is a great place to start jotting down bits and pieces of ideas for your story's plot: a confrontation with a villain, a mystery that needs to be solved, a journey into the unknown, or even self-exploration. For fun, try drawing your story ideas instead of writing them down. If your character comes from outer space, draw a sketch of a spaceship rocketing toward Earth. Like ancient cave paintings, your illustrations might get the point across before you even put words in a character's mouth.

STORY STARTERS

How do you start a story? It's a million-dollar question! You don't have to start at the beginning. Write about the parts of the story that excite you most, and build the rest of the story around those core ideas. Here's more cool brain training to build your comic book fitness.

It's About a Samurai . . . but in Space: George Lucas, creator of *Star Wars* (which has spawned toys, comics, and television shows beyond the movies), is a fan of samurai movies. He took that genre, added a pinch of Greek mythology, and then set the story in the future instead of the past. Behold! *Star Wars*! Think of a fairy tale or fable whose ending has always driven you crazy, and rewrite it the way you think it should go, or tell it anew from a particular character's point of view. Maybe a tragedy becomes a comedy, or maybe the good guy doesn't always win. There's a cool Batman–comic story called "Waiting in the Wings," which is told by the caped crusader's butler, Alfred. The comic series *Marvels* is seen through the eyes (and lens) of Phil Sheldon, a guy who photographs superheroes saving the world.

UDON ENTERTAINMENT

Name: UDON Entertainment (Erik Ko, Arnold Tsang, Ken Siu-Chong, Shane Law, Jim Zubkavich, Matt Moylan, Omar Dogan, Jeffrey Cruz, Joe Ng, Espen Grundetjern, Gonzalo Ordóñez Arias, and Long Vo)

From: Studio is based in Toronto, Ontario, Canada, but artists are from places as diverse as the United States, Australia, Norway, China, and Korea

Its Comics: *Street Fighter*, *Street Fighter Legends*, *Darkstalkers*, *Vent*, *Makeshift Miracle*, *Deadpool*, *Agent-X*, *Sentinel*, *Robotech*, *Thundercats*, and more

What was your first or favorite comic when you were younger?
Many of our crew grew up on superhero comics, but also a healthy balance of manga.

When did you know you wanted to make comics?
As soon as our studio was formed. Before that, it seemed like a pipedream.

What kinds of things inspire your comic book creations?

Amazing art and design from other artists. Video games, movies, toys—you name it. There's so much variety out there, and all of it feeds into our inspiration/motivation to create our own work.

What tools do you use to create your comics?

Most of our studio's artwork starts out as traditional line work done with pencil or ink on paper, but afterward it's formatted and colored using Photoshop. For graphic design we use InDesign and Acrobat. We're pretty Adobe reliant.

What are great ways for kids to create comics right now?

The Internet is the ultimate level playing field for people of just about any age group to post up their art and have it be seen by people from all over the place, and the tools are getting easier than ever to use. If someone is too young for posting, then creating comics is as simple as folding some paper and starting to draw. Don't be afraid, just create!

How do you use technology to create comics?

Digital painting, lettering, graphic design, formatting, color correction, file transferring, communicating, and invoicing. Technology makes our studio run smoothly and allows us to work with artists and clients from all over the world in a convenient and organized way.

Why is telling a story with comics important to you?

Comics without stories are just pinups. The mixture of words and images together in comics form a unique bond, and the result takes some of the best traits of both and makes them something else entirely.

How did making comics prepare you for a job in animation?

Many of our artists actually started in animation and migrated over to comics afterward. The skill sets for both fields have a lot in common: communication, clarity, design, and action.

How do you use social media to create or promote your work?

We have a studio website, online store, Facebook fan page, Twitter, and deviantART all working in tandem to let our fans know about new products, convention appearances, and special contests. Our deviantART page is one of the most popular in the entire dA community and has become particularly important to us as a fan outreach platform. Fans, potential clients, and fellow pros see a steady stream of new work from our artists, and it constantly reminds them of the new projects we have on deck. It's an invaluable part of our day-to-day operations.

News Flash: Watch the news and see what is going on in the world around you. Wonder Woman, one of the most patriotic superheroes ever, was created in response to World War II. Maybe you can create a story about a misfit kid who wants to form a more peaceful world. If there's an issue you have a strong opinion about, don't be afraid to voice it in your comics. They're perfect for that.

Oldies . . . but Really Goodies: Take a trip to a local comic book store and look at some of the long-running comics such as the *Fantastic Four, Superman, Batman, Uncanny X-Men, The Incredible Hulk*, and *Amazing Spider-Man*. What is it about these comics that make them great? To me, Pokémon (manga or anime) was just about collecting Tentacool and Lickilicky until my wife, who's from Japan, told me it's also about training the monsters to behave the right way (or wrong way if you're Team Rocket). Maybe you'll find inspiration in the pages of comic book classics like *Justice League, The Avengers*, or Akira Toriyama's *Dragon Ball*.

Mission Accomplished: Start your story *after* your character has accomplished his or her goal. Maybe right off the bat, Star Champ frees the people of Moon-2 and says, "The Moonians can at last taste freedom, but this scar on my cheek will forever remind me of my brother's betrayal!" Scar? Betrayal? Hold up, I didn't even know Star Champ had a brother! Or maybe over at Parent Academy—the only school run by kids for misbehaving parents—odd Mr. Otomu blurts out, "I told you I'd graduate! Bwah-ha-ha!" On the very first page, his diploma is on fire, he's got a broken flowerpot on his head, and his foot is wedged in a bee hive. I'd drop whatever I was doing to read how all that happened! What do you think? Can you give your readers the outcome first and still have them hanging around to see how it all happened?

CLIFF-HANGERS

If you're writing a continuing story that will be told over several issues, you might want to add several cliff-hangers to keep your readers coming back for more. Cliff-hangers are great for building suspense. Maybe a hero is being pursued by a villain. The villain, though, turns out to be an old friend. The readers don't learn that until the last page and have to wait to see how the story plays out in the next issue. Check out these other cliff-hanger ideas.

Matt Groening, creator of *The Simpsons*, named many of his characters after streets in his hometown of Portland, Oregon. There's Quimby, Kearney, Flanders, and more.

Escape: After pages of hot pursuit, when we finally think the hero's caught the villain for good, the villain escapes.

Dead or Alive: A main character could be left dangling—literally—at the end of an issue, leaving the readers wondering, "Will she survive?"

The Clock Is Ticking . . . : Will the hero be able to stop the vat of exploding chocolate pudding in time?! Will she save the planet before it's destroyed and *still* make it to her high school math final?!

True Identities: So, you think you finally figured out the villain's true identity? Think again! It's a clone! And the clone has a robot double! And the robot double has a hologram! Nothing is as it seems, and only your most discerning readers will get all the hidden clues.

SETTINGS

The setting or background of your comic is where your story takes place. It can be anywhere in the universe and at any point in time, real or imagined. Comic book stories usually have more than one setting. Often the setting can make or break your comic. Here are a few ideas to give your comics' landscapes some flavor.

Local Hero: Reinvent your favorite superheroes or sorcerers, but put them in *your* backyard. Not every crime fighter needs to live in New York City, and not every wizard needs to have a British accent. Take a look around you. How would a masked protector fit in with your surroundings? If there's no crime to fight, would Captain Werewolf deliver pizza instead? How would magic spells affect the "dull" world of bus stops and corner stores? Mixing a fictional character with a real, personal place is an outstanding way to learn about the history of your town, too. Share the unique customs of your local culture, just do it in an interesting, even unpredictable, way.

Scene Stealer: Think about the setting as an invisible character with emotions all its own. Where do you want the story to take place? A rowdy train station? A temperamental tropical island? Your quiet street? Then think of *specific* scenery. Do crowds of people pour out of subway cars? Does that island volcano threaten to explode? Are Martians your neighbors, fixing a spaceship behind the garage door? Check out "art-of" books from animated movies to see some vibrant, emotive landscapes: *Kung Fu Panda, Megamind, Madagascar,*

Tangled, *How to Train Your Dragon*, *Rise of the Guardians*, and *Howl's Moving Castle* are just a few.

Mise-en-scène (meez–ahn–sahn): In film terminology, there's a fancy word, *mise-en-scène*, which means "everything in its place." It's like telling a lot of your story in a single panel. For example, a mise-en-scène of a destroyed city in post–World War II Europe would let us know that the characters are living in a bleak era in history. The mise-en-scène in Cartoon Network's *Samurai Jack* cartoon lets us know what life is in the future under the rule of the villainous Aku. You might want to try creating a mise-en-scène to set a particular mood at the beginning of your story.

Still confused? Well, I'll tell you a trick. Find some old board games like Risk, Clue, or Monopoly. Your mise-en-scène is what you see when you look first at the whole board. Then, zoom in on one part of that board. That's where your character's story might begin.

Paradise, Lost and Found: Imagine a world with all of your favorite things in one place, along with all of the things that you always wished existed. What would your ideal world look like? Try the opposite of this, too. If the main character of your comic book was placed in the worst environment you could ever imagine, what would it look like?

There's an old episode of a weird television show called *Twilight Zone*, where a guy just wants to be left alone with his favorite things: books! The world ends, and he finally has time to just read and read. But when his glasses break, it's not paradise for much longer.

TREASURE CHEST

Now that you've tried out some new ideas for creative story lines, it's important to remember one thing: *Don't throw anything away.* Decorate a box—you can recycle a cardboard one—with paint and stickers. Or draw skulls and crossbones on it so that no one will spy on your ideas. Make it into a treasure chest of your imagination. You never know when you'll want to go back and use some little tidbit from one of your old stories. You might not think it's good now, but five years from now you could think it's the greatest idea ever.

SARATEP SUTHY

Age: 23

Education: Undergraduate student at Woodbury University, majoring in animation and minoring in video game design

Her Comic: *EviL Love LivE*

What are your favorite comic books?

"Fighting evil by moonlight, winning love by daylight, never running from a real fight. She's the one named Sailor Moon!" Naoko Takeuchi's *Sailor Moon* was my very first comic at eleven years old, given to me by my big sister, Jane. She took me to a comic book shop and, needless to say, *Batman* and *Spider-Man* didn't hold much appeal to a little girl. That one comic set the wheels of my future rolling.

Why do you like creating comics?

Story. There is a story that plays out in my mind, and writing it won't show the scenes that are there. There are angles, views, subtle shifts of the eyes and body language that have to be seen to be interpreted. Sometimes seeing the emotions play out hits harder than being told the character is sad.

Where do you get the inspiration for your creations?

EviL Love LivE was inspired by the antagonists in every story I have read. I wanted to make them the main characters, to see what they go through and what goes through their minds. Tricking people to root for the bad guys and boo the good guys also brings a smile to my face.

What are your favorite tools to use when writing and drawing comics?

Paper. Pencil. A good eraser. Drawing with a pencil allows more range of lines and the emotions that comes with it. I lose a lot of that when it's

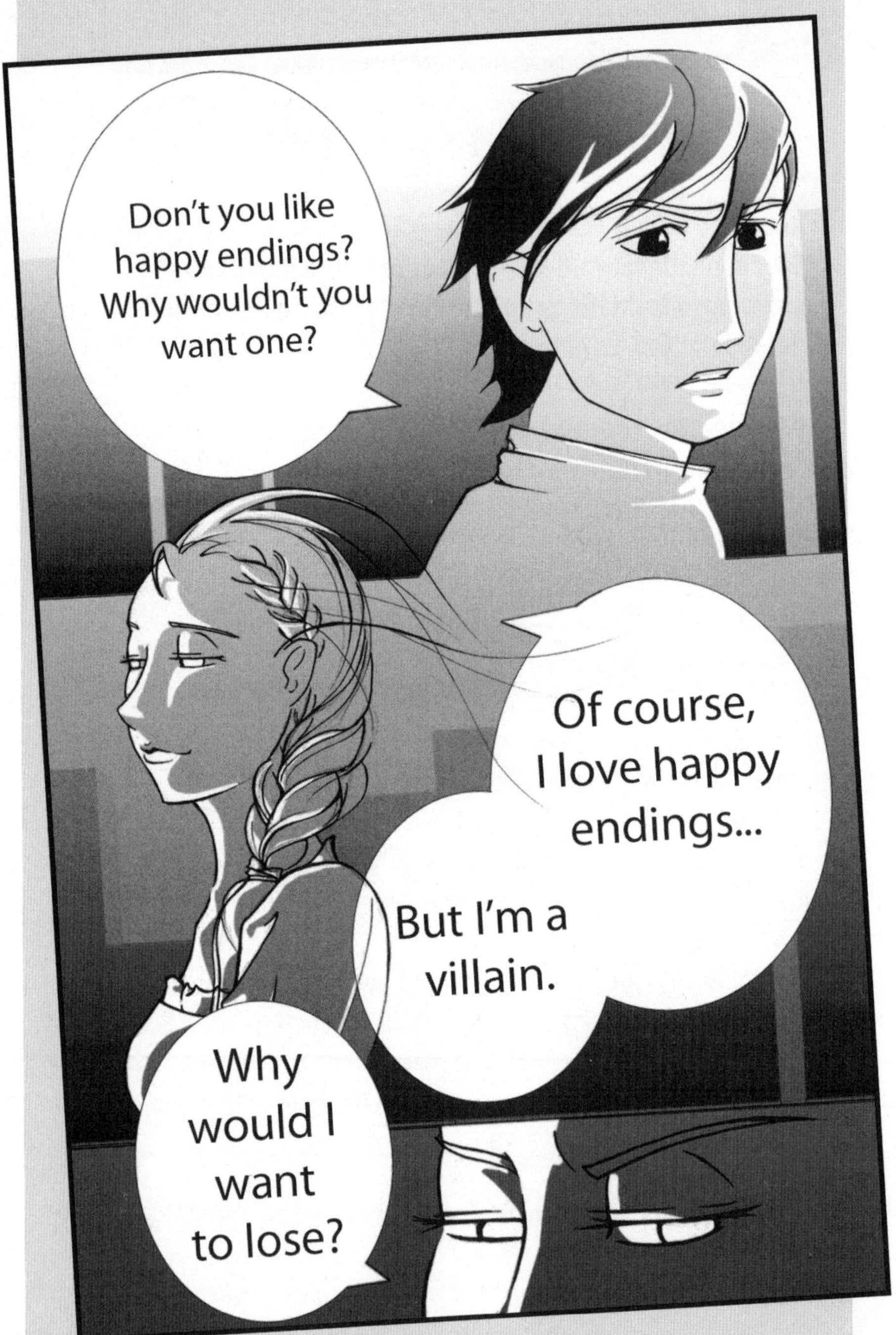

Don't you like happy endings? Why wouldn't you want one?
Of course, I love happy endings...
But I'm a villain.
Why would I want to lose?

transferred digitally and refined. I can draw on tablets, but I lose even more when I clean up the lines on something less detailed.

Does technology help you create?

Without openCanvas or Photoshop, my fingers would be full of blisters from using Micron pens to refine and clean my line work. My eye would permanently twitch from every hated line that I could not erase, that taunted me from its embedded spot on the white paper. Also, for someone who always has a pencil in her hand, my writing is only legible to me. It would be pointless for others to try and read my comics.

How do you think making comics could help you in other creative careers?

Story through art is what got me into comics, and drawing comics has gotten me to animation. Both not only tell a story, but show people things they could not imagine or picture in their own minds.

What are your plans for the future?

I want to rule the world. Maybe not this one, but an animated one will do just as well. Becoming an animator and creating characters and worlds people want to fall into is my biggest goal.

What's the best advice you can give your peers?

Listen to the criticism of all, but only follow the ones that are actually helpful.

LAYOUT: PUTTING IT ALL TOGETHER

Before you launch a full-fledged comic book, you'll need to break down your illustrations and story ideas into several steps: scripting your comic, drawing thumbnails, creating penciled pages, inking your work, creating a cover, and choosing a title.

SCRIPTING YOUR COMIC

Because comic book stories are told almost entirely through dialogue, you will need to write a script for your comic book before you illustrate it, just like you would if you were writing a play. Good dialogue should be interesting, tell you something about the characters, and advance the plot. Because much of the comic book story can be told through the characters' expressions and body language, your characters' conversations can be brief and to the point. You can use sound effects (also called onomatopoeia) like *zap! crunch!* and *sproing!* to jazz up the action when no real words are needed.

The following is a script excerpt from *Barry Onyx and the Dino-Finders*, created by me and the supertalented Jack Pollock. It's an example of what your script might look like. Notice the scene descriptions, dialogue, sound effects, and captions.

• •

Sample Page from a *Barry Onyx* Script

PAGE 1

PANEL 1
Stegosaurus in foreground, head-to-body shot. In background, Barry and Tyra small, hiding behind prehistoric foliage.

BARRY: So, Tyra, what do you think is going on here?

TYRA: You mean, what do I *see*, Mr. Onyx?

PANEL 2
Close-up on Tyra and Barry, still hiding behind foliage, looking at off-panel Stega.

BARRY: Not exactly. I mean, what's *happening*?

PANEL 3
Close-up on Stega's tail whipping around, maybe perforating some big low-lying leaves as he does.

TYRA (CAPTION): That stegosaurus's spiked tail is movin' like crazy! He's defending himself!

PANEL 4

Rex in foreground, running toward reader. Stega in mid-ground, pissed off, but too far away to hurt Rex. Rex has a goofy, tongue-wagging look on his face, playing up the comedy, downplaying the danger.

REX: It's a Thagomizer, Tyra!

LINK: Don'cha wanna play fetch, big guy? Sheesh!

TYRA (OFF): Teach him "sit" and "stay" *first*, Rex! Haha!

SKETCHING THUMBNAILS

Your script is just the start. The next step is changing all your scene descriptions from text to art. To help map out your comic page, you might first want to draw some thumbnail sketches for each panel. Thumbnails are quick, loose sketches that you draw before you begin the penciled page. Artists use thumbnails to sketch out character positions, perspectives, and light sources *before* they draw a comics page. Thumbnail layouts are great because you can change a panel without having to redo your whole comic from

Hergé, creator of *Tintin*, is a household name in Belgium. He's been awarded the Grand Prix Saint-Michel, is in the Eisner Award and Harvey Award Halls of Fame, and even has an asteroid named after him.

scratch. When Jack does *Barry Onyx* thumbnails, he's thinking about how to use the characters and setting to best tell the story.

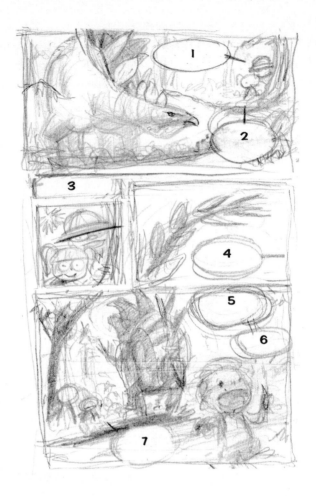

Ready to try some thumbnails? Using one of your completed scripts, draw a rough, quick sketch to correspond with each panel in your script. This shouldn't take long. When you're done, you will have a set of thumbnails outlining your comic sequence.

DRAWING THE PANELS

Once you've finished your thumbnails, you can illustrate the penciled pages using your thumbnails as a guide. Take your time! Professional comics artists draw about one to four pages per week, on average. Between each panel, leave about a quarter of an inch of white space for the gutter. Focus on drawing your characters and setting first, and position balloons or captions later, trying not to cover too much art.

INKING

Inking your comics can take some time to master at first. Here's a tip: The more you practice using your brush and inking in your sketchbook, the better it will look on your comics page. Dip the brush gently into the ink bottle. You may want to try a couple of test lines on a separate piece of paper before you ink your penciled illustrations. Draw very lightly at first to get a feel for the width of the brush. It's different from a rigid pencil, right? The more you practice, the more you'll notice the amazing range the brush offers. Don't worry if you make a mistake—it's easy to make corrections with white correction fluid after the ink dries. Here is an example of the same page from *Barry Onyx and the Dino-Finders*, in finished form.

RUDY SPIESSERT

From: Nice, France
Job: Comic books artist
His Comics: *Ingmar*, *Hélas*, *Les Villes d'un Jour*, *Space Warped*

What was your first or favorite comic when you were younger?

Spirou and Fantasio, which I used to read in *Le Journal de Spirou* [now just *Spirou*], the oldest French-speaking comics magazine still alive. I was also a great fan of the Lucky Luke series by Morris and Goscinny. Some of those [issues], like *Tortillas for the Daltons*, are still among my all-time favorites.

When did you know you wanted to make comics?

Around the age of eight. I started copying my favorite comics heroes and became rather good at it—I even sold some drawings on the playground. My goal at this time was to draw the cover of *Le Journal de Spirou*, which finally happened in 2007, so now I can die in peace (but not immediately, if possible).

What kinds of things inspire your comic book creations?

Newspapers, movies, TV, other comics, real life … everything. I think about it *all the time*—it is more a behavior disorder than a working technique. I probably should ask a psychiatrist about that, but if he cures me, I will lose my job.

What tools do you use to create your comics?

Sometimes pencils and paper and sometimes a Wacom tablet, depends on the mood. When I was younger, I used to try many tools and techniques; now that I am wise and venerable I know that only the result matters. This is particularly true with humorous comics, in which the drawings have to be efficient, first of all.

Ooga-Booga © Rudy Spiessert

What are great ways for kids to create comics right now?
It may sound terribly old-fashioned, but for me the recipe is still the same: good ideas and a lot of work. The only (big) difference with their generation is that their creations may be easily broadcast through the internet.

How do you use technology to create comics?
Search engines are convenient for the documentation, and graphic software allows [you] to work faster, but fundamentally it has no influence on my work.

Why is telling a story with comics important to you?
There are two questions: Why telling stories? Because I realized very soon that real life was boring. Why with comics? Probably because it is the only thing I manage to do properly.

How do you use social media to create or promote your work?
The answer is short: I don't. I hope to become someday the very last man on Earth not to be on Facebook.

DESIGNING YOUR COVER

The cover is a dynamic piece of your comic book. Use it to draw the reader into your world. There are lots of amazing comics illustrators who have designed great covers—*Scott Pilgrim* creator Bryan Lee O'Malley is good at it—and you might want to look at some of their work for inspiration. If you want a quick way to do a cover composition, try a close-up of the main character's head. Or use a mystical symbol from your wizard's prized spell book. Whatever you decide to draw for the cover, make sure it's intriguing enough so that people will want to pick up your comic and read it. It's really a marketing piece, so think about how to best draw people in. Also think about how and where people might see your book out in the real world, and consider what your cover composition will look like shrunk down online, in print, and reproduced in black and white (which could happen if it gets reviewed in a newspaper, magazine, or blog). Keeping the design simple will help it stay more readable in different formats.

FINISH LINE!

You've written an awesome script and have been drawing in your sketchbook like there's no tomorrow. Now it's time to get crackin' on your very first comic book pages. Keep things loose. Don't try to perfect the pages too much. The first pages you ever do don't need to look too refined. Try to enjoy every part of drawing: the thumbnails, the pencils, the inks, the lettering, and the coloring. If you're not feeling it, do something that you know will put you there. Dip into your favorite comic, music, movie, or game. Pet an animal you love. Do anything that makes you happy, and especially do those things that inspire you to create. For some people, just the act of sitting down in their studio is enough to put them in a good mood. In any case, a healthy, excited attitude is more important than artistic perfection. Try to sit down in your studio with a big smile on your face, and have fun creating your own comic—it's one of the best feelings in the world.

ANGELA FERNOT

Age: 24
Education: Associate's degree in fine art, currently a student at The Kubert School
Her Comic: *Legends of the Owl Queen*

What are your favorite comic books?

That's hard to say. Now I mostly collect comics that have really good artwork and even better storytelling, because I want to study them and be inspired. However, there are a few that I love for everything from the art to the writing. At the moment my list includes titles like *Blacksad*; *Winterworld*; *Batman: Hush*; *Off Road*; *Joe the Barbarian*; *Walking Dead*; and *Dong Xoai, Vietnam 1965*.

Why do you like creating comics?

I like to create because it's a challenge. I am always pushing myself to find better ways to tell a story or draw a panel. And truthfully, my favorite comics have inspired me so much that I want to create something that will inspire someone else the same way.

Where do you get the inspiration for your creations?

Everywhere. Everything around me has the potential to inspire new ideas. I also look at everything from Greek sculptures to Disney animations to other comic books. The stories that I'm working on now were inspired by reading owl legends from around the world.

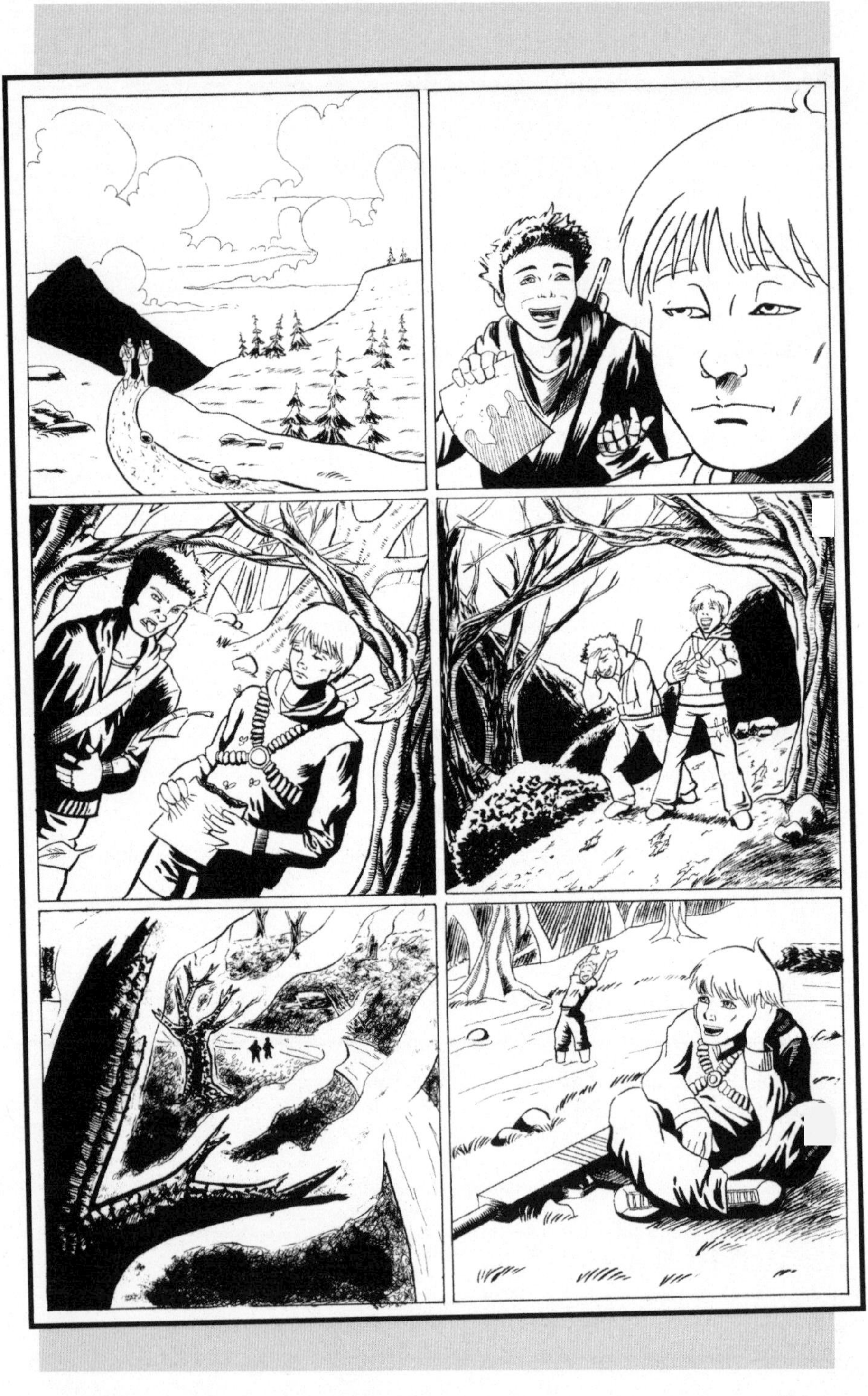

What are your favorite tools to use when writing and drawing comics?

When writing I use the internet a lot, and I usually end up surrounded by bits of paper with sketches and ideas written all over them. When drawing I try to stay completely traditional and use pencils, brushes, quills, pens, and occasionally some random objects for texture. My coloring is all done digitally in Photoshop.

Does technology help you create?

Technology has made things a lot easier for me than for my predecessors. All of my lettering is done on the computer now. Mistakes are easily fixable because of my ability to scan my pages and edit them in Photoshop. And best of all, everything can be done much faster now.

How do you think making comics could help you in other creative careers?

One of the most important elements of telling a story is communicating clearly. Advertising, graphic design, storyboarding, and many other jobs require that exact same thing. Plus, working in comics requires being fast, determined, and able to meet deadlines. Those are good qualities for any job.

What are your plans for the future?

Some day I hope to publish my work. I have a long way to go, but I am confident that I'll make it happen.

What's the best advice you can give your peers?

Don't ever give up. We all have bad days—bad weeks, even. But I have learned that to persevere is to succeed where others could not. Oh, and practice anatomy and perspective like your life depends on it!

COPY-SHOP COMICS

Do you think you have to wait until you're older or until you're discovered by a major comic book publisher to make comics? Think again. You can mass-produce ingenious comics right now that will impress other comics fans and provide exposure for your work.

Kids across the country are writing, drawing, creating, and even selling their own comics, so why should you wait? With a copier, it's easy to put together your own comics cheaply.

BARGAIN-BASEMENT COMICS

At comics conventions, I talk to artists a lot. I am amazed—and pleasantly surprised—by how many travel down the self-publishing route. They liked making comics and weren't going to wait for the *Batman* editor to call them (though that's cool, too). At Japan's

Comiket convention, "artist alley" is lined with *mangaka* (comics artists) devoted to their own characters and stories. Nothing stopped them, and nothing will stop you from publishing your own comic—get it hot off the presses from your local copy shop.

Though self-published artists spend a certain amount of time and money printing their own comics, creating your own comic can be inexpensive. How much money you want to spend on your creation is up to your budget. If it costs ten cents for each copy of your homemade comic, you might want to sell each for twenty-five cents or more. If you're only trying to get exposure for your work and spread the word, you might want to spend as little as possible, with quality still in mind, and give copies out for free.

COPY-SHOP CREATION

Making comics on a copy machine is one of the easiest ways to make a quick comic. All you need is your artwork and a basic budget. Copy shops have the rest: staplers, glue, scissors, rulers, and different papers for the inside and the cover.

Assemble Your Master Manuscript

Comics generally have these elements:

Front cover: You should include title and bylines (Written and Illustrated by _____). You might also include a subtitle or series name.

Front matter: Somewhere near the front, often on the inside of the cover or on the first inside left page, you should list yourself and any cocreators as the copyright holders and add the year of publication (check a published comic book or graphic novel for the right format). This makes a statement of ownership for your work, and even if no one ever steals your ideas, it's worthwhile to you to have a reminder of when and where you created this piece. Adding your phone number or email can be helpful if you plan to submit these for publication. You might also include the name of your studio and the town where you live.

Body: This is the beginning, middle, and end of your story. The story usually begins on the first right-hand page.

Back matter: Sometimes the back of comics includes a teaser (a short excerpt) or a blurb (quote from someone who's read your comic) from or about the next installment of a series or other books by the same creators. Graphic novels often include a short author bio in the back as well.

Back cover: Some people put the copyright information or ad card here. Published comics often have ads, so you could create fake ones or advertise something of interest to you. On a graphic novel, information about the creator might be on the back cover.

Get Printing

Stick with a piece of 8½-by-11 inch paper since it's the size of paper at copy shops. It's easy to bind, and you don't have to do any fancy trimming to a smaller size. You can also fold it in half to double the number of pages in your comic.

1. Carefully gather up your completed original artwork for your story. It doesn't matter how many pages—your story could be eight, sixteen, twenty-two, or two hundred pages if you've *really* been busy! Make sure you have a cover image, too, as well as a title.
2. At the copy shop, make one master copy of your artwork. Use the master to produce the other copies, so you don't have to keep using your original artwork. Make sure all the pages are in the right order, too. Depending on the size of your original art, you may have to reduce it on the copier to fit. A clerk can help, but if your drawings are on typical art board, you have to reduce it by about 60 percent to fit an 8½-by-11 inch sheet of paper.

3. Once you have a master copy, choose your paper and start making copies. Inexpensive, standard white copy paper is great for the interior pages of your comic. Colored paper can be nice for the cover but is not necessary. Just be sure that the colors aren't too dark—you want people to be able to read your comic.

4. When you're done, there are lots of ways to bind your comic together. The easiest and cheapest is to fold it in half. This idea is great for keeping the cost down—though your readers might tend to lose a page here and there. Adding one or two staples should help keep your comic book in one piece. And there you have it—a bound comic to sell or give to family and friends!

The copy-shop staff might have some good suggestions and advice, so ask them for help. They can offer assistance and estimate the cost to produce what you have in mind *before* you start making copies, show you how to use some of the tools, and introduce you to some promotional ideas, too, like iron-ons of your characters for T-shirts, printings on magnets, etc. Depending on your budget and the amount of copies you want, sometimes copying in bulk can make a cheaper per-comic cost. Bulk rates sometimes include folding and stapling but, of course, doing that yourself is usually the easiest way to save some cash.

J. BONE

From: A small town in Ontario, Canada
Job: Freelance comic book artist and illustrator
His Comics: *Solar Stella, Alison Dare: Little Miss Adventures, Mutant Texas, X-Statix, Spider-Man: Tangled Web, The Spirit, Super Friends, Retroactive: Wonder Woman*

Alison Dare © J. Bone and J. Torres, published by Tundra books, 2010

What was your first or favorite comic when you were younger?

I used to buy used comic books from an old bookseller in my home town. My favorites were any books with the Metal Men (usually *The Brave and the Bold*) and Hot Stuff (Harvey Comics). I would also regularly sign out *Asterix* and *Obelix* and *Tintin* from the local library.

When did you know you wanted to make comics?

Not until my second year in college did I start thinking about a career in comic books. I'd just discovered Mike Mignola through his *Dracula* movie adaptation and then collected all of his older work. It was also around then that he started *Hellboy*. I met a bunch of like-minded comic book fans in college, and we would introduce each other to new artists we'd discovered, which, in turn, inspired us to start making our own comic books.

What kinds of things inspire your comic book creations?

Everyday life inspires me to tell stories but almost always through some sort of science-fiction filter. I read a lot of sci-fi. Sometimes a story idea comes from wanting to explore a different story path than the one in the book I've just read. Or to parody what I've read (finding the funny in a serious, straightforward sci-fi story).

What tools do you use to create your comics?

Penciling is done with a regular HB pencil. Inking with either Faber-Castell Pitt pens or a brush and Speedball ink (all depending on deadlines and what I feel like working with at the time). All of my coloring is done in Photoshop.

What are great ways for kids to create comics right now?

The best way to create comics is to just draw. Use whatever paper you've got available and any drawing tools. (It doesn't have to be what the professionals use.)

How do you use technology to create comics?

I use Photoshop to color my work, and to scan my inks, which I then send digitally to my editor. I'm about to learn InDesign so that I can put my own books together for, eventually, self-publication. I still draw traditionally, but I've recently started doing my rough thumbnails using a drawing tablet.

Why is telling a story with comics important to you?

I like the control I have when telling stories with comics. As the artist, everything on the page is my work. In film terms, I get to be all of the characters, choose the costuming, decorate the sets and locations, and direct the action. I love playing around with all of those aspects when I'm drawing a book.

How did making comics prepare you for a job in animation?

Actually, I worked in reverse—right out of college I got a job at an animation company doing location and prop design. Drawing locations every day for three years taught me a lot of shortcuts for drawing in perspective, which I use in my comic book drawing all the time. I learned the importance of drawing a "real" environment for your characters to bring believability to your story.

How do you use social media to create or promote your work?

I have a few blogs for various aspects of my artwork. Right now I don't know if I'm using them to their full potential. Mainly I post new drawings, pages, or sketches from current projects and use the comments section to talk to my blog followers and fans.

SIGNATURE DESIGNS

There are many ways you can give your comics that personal, homemade touch. You can make your comics unique by autographing them, but here are a few other ideas for making a rare comic book created specifically for your readers.

Interaction: Create a mystery comic that the reader has to solve by posing a question at the end of each page, such as, "If you think the robot butler filled the bathtub with chocolate sauce, turn to page 9. If you think the circus clown did it, turn to page 12." Let the reader determine the direction of the story. The story will be different for each person reading it.

Sketchbook Book: You can use sketches from your idea journal for your comic book. Make copies of the best pages, and bind them into a limited-edition book. Every month or so, do a new volume of your sketchbook—for back-to-school, Halloween, or best yet, National Comic Book Day (September 25). Give them to friends and family first, maybe your art teacher, or pop one in the mail to a comics company, and see what they think; editors are often pretty cool about getting back to kids. Make sets for yourself that chronicle your best comics and sketches from the year, and archive it. (That means keep it forever, like a reference book in the library.)

Mix Master: Cut pictures and phrases out of magazines and newspapers, glue in pieces of fabric, or color paper by hand to make the comics pop right off the page. This way, each reader gets a comic you made by hand just for her. If you know the person well, you can personalize the comic with things you know he'll like.

Best Mini-Comic Ever: Andi Watson is the creator of comics like *Skeleton Key*, *Breakfast After Noon*, *Slow News Day*, and now *Glister*. I dig his format for cool mini-comics. Follow the instructions and diagram below to make your own.

1. Choose a piece of white paper, and trim the paper to 8¼ inches wide by 5¾ inches high.
2. Fold the paper in half, lengthwise. Next, fold it in half again, but this time widthwise. Then fold it one more time, widthwise.
3. Now unfold the paper, and lay it flat. You should have eight rectangles marked by the folds (see Example A).

Each rectangle represents one of your panels. With your scissors, cut a slit in the center margin that separates the four panels in the center of the page (follow the dotted lines in Example A for your cut). Cut *only* this section.

4. Use each panel in your mini-comic to illustrate your story. Only illustrate one side of the paper. Note: Make sure that the tops of your characters' bodies are at the top of each panel; the tops point toward the center margin (see Example B).

5. When your illustrations are complete, fold the paper again lengthwise (see Example C). Your art should be facing out with the blank side of the paper facing in. With your fingers on the four center panels—two on each side of the fold—create an x shape with the paper as if you're looking at it from above (see Example D). Then fold it so that the shape resembles an open book.

6. Now press the paper flat, like you're closing a book (see Example E). You should have a mini-comic book! If you unfold the paper and lay it flat again, you can bring it to the copy shop, where you can copy as many comics as you want on different colors of paper. When you get home, trim and fold the copies up in the exact same way to make tons more mini-comics. Put your name and contact info

on the back cover so people can get in touch with you if they want more comics.

Example C

Example D

Example E

That's it: Six easy steps to creating your own mini-comic that you can give as gifts, trade, mail, and use to promote and display your work. Before you know it, you'll have people waiting in line for the next story.

Comics Company: Invite a group of friends over to keep you company for a comic book brainstorming session. Maybe one of you has a fantastic character idea but doesn't know how to fit it into a story. Perhaps you have been working out a storyline for the past few weeks but just can't seem to draw the right character. Talking and drawing with friends might be just the thing to clear your writer's block or get you out of a story jam. Produce a comic with a group of friends who share your creative spirit, and you'll be stunned by the results.

Postcard Comics: One of my favorite ideas is making postcards into comic strips. Find out from the post office how much a standard postcard costs and what the maximum size can be. You should be able to fit two postcards on one piece of 8½-by-11 paper, with trimming. (Be sure to use heavier paper, like cardstock.)

The first postcard is the first panel of art, and the second postcard picks up the story from the first. Make ten copies of your art at the copy shop, and ask a clerk to trim each to individual postcard size. You'll be left with ten copies of each postcard. Send out the first one to friends, neighbors, other artists, editors, and publishers the first week. The next week, send out the second. Keep doing this as long as you like. You may have a suspense-filled story that runs for weeks or even months ... all on a series of handy postcards. If sending postcards through the mail is too old-fashioned for you, you can do the same thing by scanning your art and sending it as a PDF attachment to an email.

MASINA KIM

Age: 10
Education: Fifth-grade student
Her Comic: *Suki N. Moss and the Spaceship*

What are your favorite comic books?

My favorite comic book series is *Big Nate*, but my favorite authors are Sharon Creech, Gitty Daneshvari, and Sienna Mercer.

Why do you like creating comics?

I like creating comic books because I always have an idea for a story, but when I try to make it into a book I always get bored quickly. Comic books are quick and easier to make for me. When I have my story already written in a comic, I can one day make it into a book.

Where do you get the inspiration for your creations?

I don't really get my inspiration from anywhere—I just draw. When I want to draw a person, I start with the head or the eyes; then I add to it. When I want to draw an animal, I start with a sketch of a horizontal oval shape.

What are your favorite tools to use when writing and drawing comics?

I always start with an outline with a regular pencil; then I add color with color pencils. When I draw, I like to draw with shades of gray and black, but on spots like an eye, I like to add a little green.

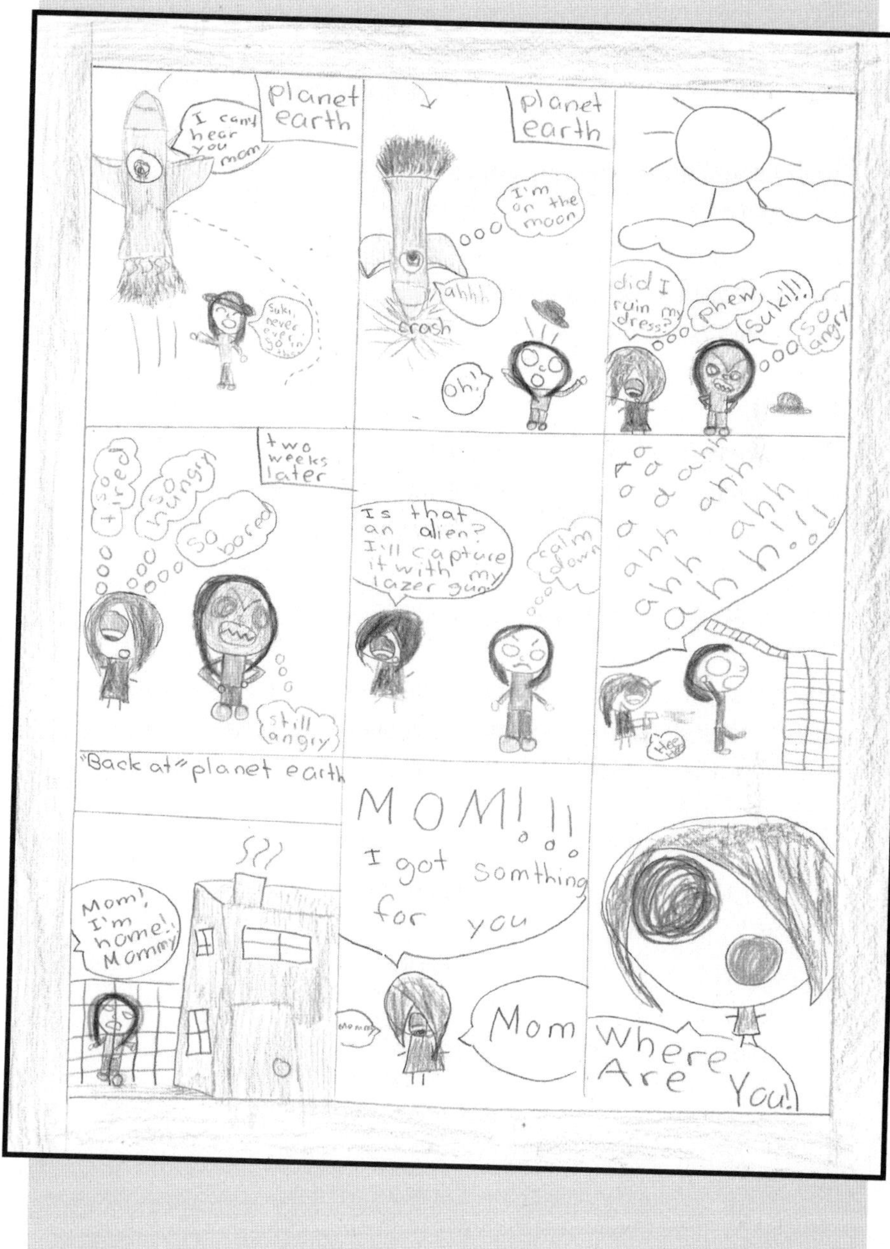
planet earth
I can't hear you mom
planet earth
I'm on the moon
ahhh
crash
oh!
did I ruin my dress?
phew
Suki!!
so angry
two weeks later
so tired
so hungry
so bored
still angry
Is that an alien? I'll capture it with my lazer gun
calm down
ahh ahh ahh ahh ahh ahh ahh!!!
"Back at" planet earth
Mom! I'm home!! Mommy
MOM!!!
I got somthing for you
Mom
Where Are You!!

Does technology help you create?

I usually keep all my drawings in a phone. When I want to see them, I just go on to the phone and do whatever I want with them. I like playing with the pictures on the phone because on there is an app where I can change the brightness, contrast, blurriness, and pixels of the picture.

How do you think making comics could help you in other creative careers?

Making these comic books helps me with my drawing and writing skills. I like drawing a lot, and when I can make the pictures better, it helps me feel more proud of my work. Comics are fun to make, so when I'm practicing my writing skills, it doesn't feel like work.

What are your plans for the future?

In the future, I would like to publish all my comics into one or a few books. When I grow up, I would like to be an author of all kinds of books.

What's the best advice you can give your peers?

The best advice I can give to my friends is that your first comic book may not be the best, but if you keep making them, they will get better and better. Also that if you see someone else's character or writing style, you can get inspiration, but you shouldn't copy because it's not your own work. Also, not all comics have to be funny.

SELF-PROMOTION: GETTING PUBLICITY FOR YOUR WORK

In your backpack, you have your first comic. It's so new, the ink is still wet. But what do you do with it? How do you get the word out to all your future fans?

Comic book publishers, like the ones listed in chapter 11: Resources, spend money to get the word out about their newest projects, but there are several easy and inexpensive ways to get exposure for your comics without investing a lot of time or money. Here are clever strategies that you can employ to market and distribute your comic.

Art Contests: One great way to get exposure for your comics is to enter art contests as often as you can. It's good practice, and you sometimes can even win prizes and awards. Comicbookresources.com runs art contests from time to time. Local comic stores do it, too (check chapter 11 for more).

Bookstore Bound: There are independent bookstores and comics shops from East Coast to West Coast devoted to small-press comics and zines. If there's a bookstore like this in your town, ask the owner or manager if she is willing to carry your comics. Even if the owner can't sell them, he might have a freebie table where you can leave a stack for anyone who wants one. The Million Year Picnic, my boyhood comic shop in Cambridge, Massachusetts, has an area right outside the store for stuff like that.

Giveaways: You can also make giveaways based on your comic book characters. For my comic *Sky Ape*, my publisher made a one-of-a-kind handmade Sky Ape stuffed animal and raffled it off to one lucky reader. We also relabeled Hershey's chocolate nuggets with Sky Ape art and called them Monkey Nuggets.

Hangin' Around: If your local comic store or coffee shop does art exhibitions, ask if you could display some of your original artwork in the store. Schools are also a fantastic place to display your work. Perhaps your art teacher can help coordinate a comic book art show or hallway exhibit. An ice-cream shop I know lets local artists put their work up for a week, and if people like it, it stays up even longer.

SANFORD GREENE

From: Columbia, South Carolina
Job: Freelance illustrator, concept artist
His Comics: *Spider-man, Hulk, X-Men, Legion of Super-Heroes*

What was your first or favorite comic when you were younger?
My first comic when I was younger was *The Avengers*. I forget what issue,

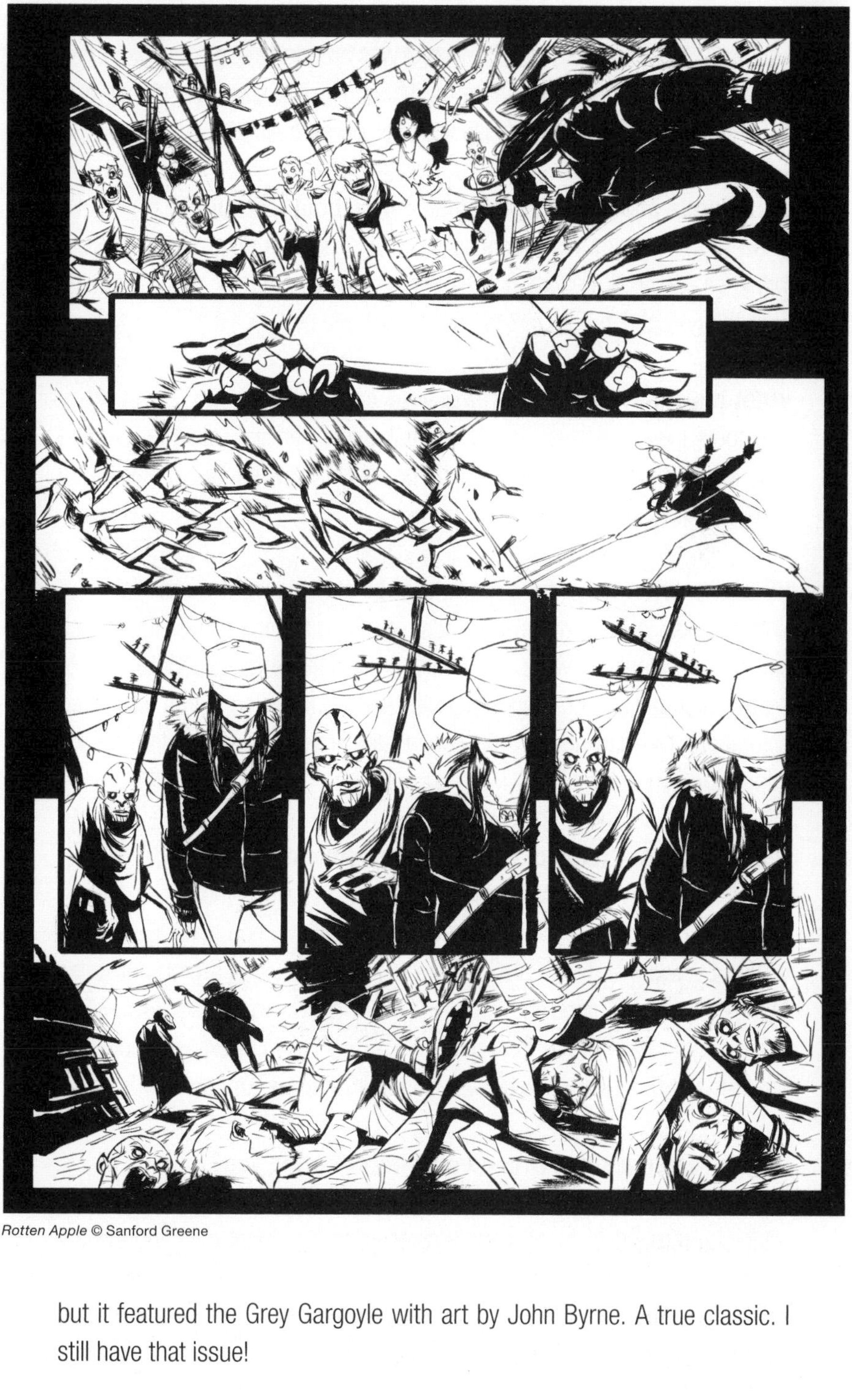

Rotten Apple © Sanford Greene

but it featured the Grey Gargoyle with art by John Byrne. A true classic. I still have that issue!

When did you know you wanted to make comics?

I knew I wanted to make comics when I was around twelve years old. I had started to collect and bring them to school. I would show my friends and draw characters from them. I was the cool kid for a while.

What kinds of things inspire your comic book creations?

I have a wide range of influences when it comes to my art. The biggest influence is urban culture. I love the style and attitude of it. Then it's European art and culture, anime, sci-fi, and Disney.

What tools do you use to create your comics?

The tools I use are Nos. 3 and 5 mechanical pencils. I also use Pentel brushes, sumi ink, Strathmore Bristol board (11 by 17). I use Photoshop to do digital coloring.

What are great ways for kids to create comics right now?

With the way technology is used today, creating art and design for comics can be done multiple ways. Photoshop is by far the most popular way to create illustrations. The program could be used for coloring and for limited animation. You can also create comics the traditional way. With comics paper and pencils and ink.

How do you use technology to create comics?

I use Photoshop with my Wacom tablet. The tablet allows me to edit illustrations that have been scanned and saved into Photoshop. I do illustrations with the Wacom as well. I also started to learn the use of a program called Manga Studio. It's good for doing line work similar to pencils and inking. One final program I'm excited about is PenTool SAI. I'm excited about this program but don't know enough about it just yet to be confident in using it.

Why is telling a story with comics important to you?

To me storytelling is the greatest element of comic book art. You must understand mood, setting, camera movement, etc. Most good storytellers in the comic book industry are great artists. I try to study some great storytellers such as Al Williamson, Jim Holdaway, John Buscema. The better your storytelling, the better your art.

How do you use social media to create or promote your work?
I use Facebook, deviantART, and my blog mainly to promote my appearances, update my current projects, and post some of my latest creations. I try to be consistent with my updates on each of these social outlets. You can contact me or check out my works on sanfordgreene.com, greenestreet.deviantart.com, or facebook.com/sanfordgreene.

Extra Credit: Do you know someone who owns a local pizza place, bakery, or take-out restaurant? Make up a stack of mini-comics and ask if he'd mind putting one in every take-out bag or box. Every month, do a new mini-comic that continues the story from the previous one. You'll have a whole bunch of hooked fans just waiting for the next exciting issue. A great time to do it is in May, around Free Comic Book Day (first Saturday in May), because people may be looking forward to free comics, but they will be surprised to get one in a place they never expected.

The Green Lantern in the movie isn't the superhero's only design. Martin Nodell created a golden age Green Lantern who had a purple cape and red shirt and boots. He hung around with Gardner Fox's golden age Flash, who wore a silver helmet with gold wings on the side. (Many people break down the history of American comics by ages, with the golden age being the earliest, and starting with the creation of Superman.)

Cause and Effect: If you can get your comics out there and help a good cause, so much the better. Mike Maihack,

creator of *Cleopatra in Space*, helped raise money for a non-profit organization that rescues Siamese cats by donating half the proceeds of his Marvel cats prints to them. Dozens of comics artists and animators, from Steve Purcell to Scott Campbell, have donated their work to the Totoro Forest Project, an effort to preserve Sayama Forest in Japan (inspiration for the *My Neighbor Totoro* anime). Got a local cause that needs defending? Chances are it'd love an artist to help it get the word out and raise funds.

Promote Yourself: Promoting your comics can be as much fun as making the comic itself. Chances are you'll have ideas to publicize your work that no one has ever done. Be creative.

Use the resources around you right now. Go easy on your budget. Personalize comics with your signature. Draw original sketches on envelopes or small paper bags, and put the comic inside as a gift. You can do a lot with simple materials, passion, and imagination. Basically, be innovative and thrifty.

Jack Kirby, responsible for creating and popularizing some of the biggest Marvel Comics characters ever, got his start working for Will Eisner, another comics legend, who created *The Spirit*.

Publishing Party: This is the best part of the whole comic book–making process, because you finally get to see all your hard work in a final product. It doesn't matter how you make your first comic, whether it's a copy-shop comic, a mini-comic, or something else entirely. Whatever it is, be proud of your creation. Treat yourself to a banana split. Splurge on a double cheeseburger. Better yet, invite a few close friends over, order a few pizzas or set up a hot-dog bar, and have them check out your work. They'll feel like they're in an exclusive club, and their word of mouth will help your cause. Be sure to document the event with photographs, which is great if you've decided to make a website or blog for your work.

There are thousands of ways to promote your work. Always keep a few mini-comics with you. If you go to a comic book convention, pass them out to potential fans. You can easily use mini-comics as business cards by including your contact information on the back cover. Before you know it, you'll have your very own die-hard fans, and your work will have a good chance of getting into the hands of editors and publishers who could eventually hire you.

WESLEY ST. CLAIRE

Age: 23
Education: Student at The Kubert School
His Comic: *Nasser of Aban*

What are your favorite comic books?

At the moment I'm mostly impressed by the book *Blacksad* by Juan Diaz Canales (writer) and Juanjo Guarnido (artist). It's written very well, and the art is fantastic. It has very good story telling, and I loved the characters.

Why do you like creating comics?

Growing up I had an overactive imagination, and I would always want to draw out what I was thinking. I just wanted to see my thoughts in front of me as if they were real, and I couldn't do that with just one picture, I had to draw out many pictures. When I got old enough to understand what comics were I knew that was what I wanted to do. In other words I love telling stories.

Where do you get the inspiration for your creations?

I was very much into fantasy, sci-fi, and kung fu movies and still am. I like bringing the reader out of an ordinary setting so they feel like they are in another world. [Artists who do this well are] Moebius for example, Akira Toriyama is another. Movies like *Blade Runner, Starship Troopers, The Fifth Element, Willow, Legend,* and so forth, those are my kind of thing.

What are your favorite tools to use when writing and drawing comics?

My favorite tools to use when writing and drawing are a .5 HB mechanical lead pencil, a .9 HB mechanical pencil, a No.2 Raphael brush, a 102 quill pen, Microns, and my computer.

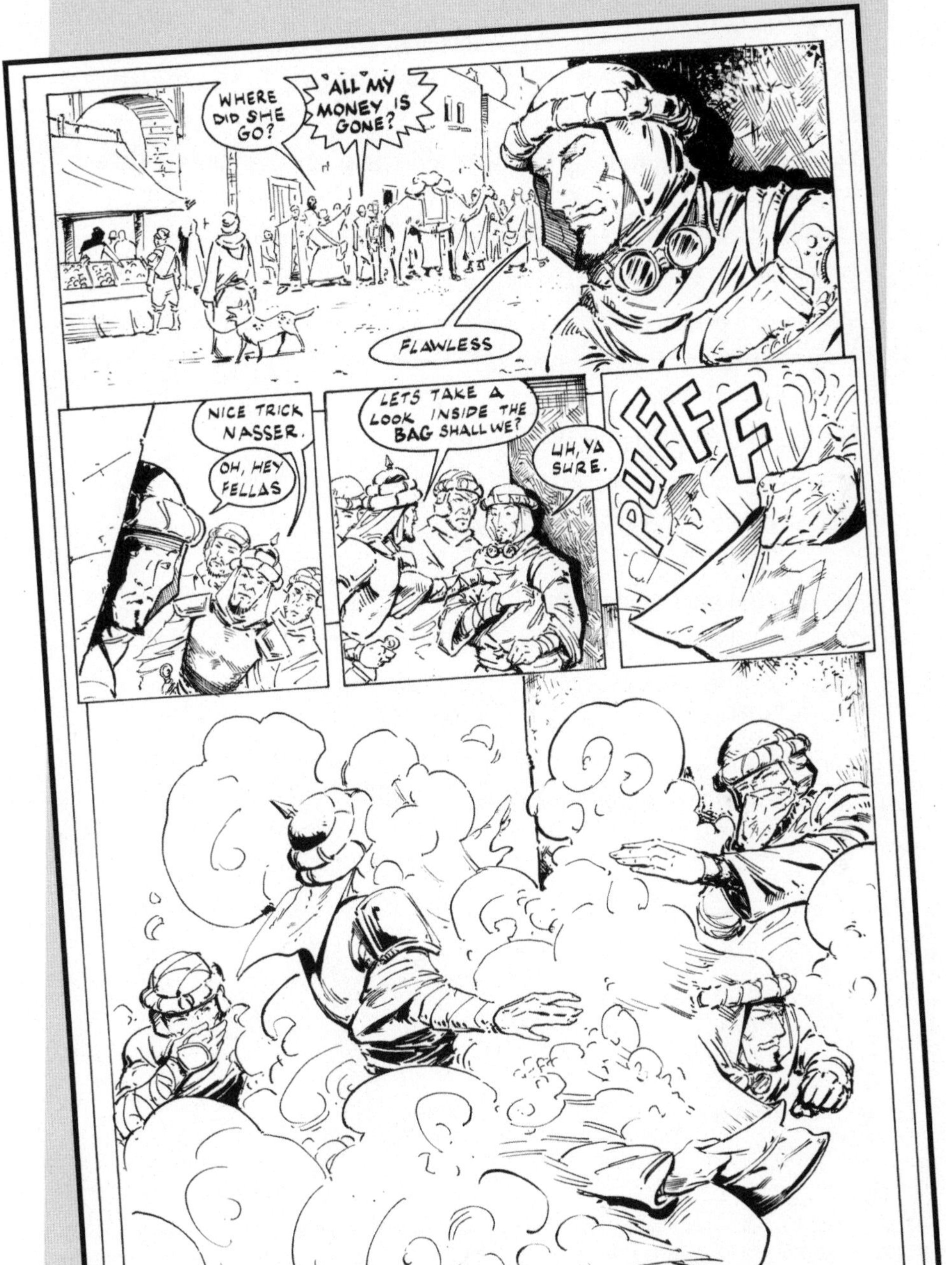
WHERE DID SHE GO?
ALL MY MONEY IS GONE?
FLAWLESS
NICE TRICK NASSER.
OH, HEY FELLAS
LETS TAKE A LOOK INSIDE THE BAG SHALL WE?
UH, YA SURE.
PUFFF

Does technology help you create?

I really only use my computer to look up references, and I use Photoshop for color and minor corrections.

How do you think making comics could help you in other creative careers?

I think making comics can help especially in moviemaking. Essentially a comic artist is a director. Comic artists choose where the camera goes and how to light certain shots. If the characters in a comic were alive we would have to tell them how to act and react.

What are your plans for the future?

I'm concentrating on finishing school and looking for work from DC and Marvel before I publish my own comic.

What's the best advice you can give your peers?

To all aspiring artists, draw from life. Draw your friends, draw your family, draw your toys, draw your pets, draw anything you see. The more you draw what's in front of you, the easier drawing becomes. Drawing things from your mind is drawing from your memory, so draw from life to build that memory, and drawing will become a piece of cake.

PORTFOLIOS: SUBMITTING YOUR COMICS TO PUBLISHERS

You've been working hard making your own comics, filling your sketchbook with great ideas, and creating comics with friends. But what's next? How do you get from there to working on your favorite comic for a big publisher?

When I was a kid, my cousin sent for art submissions guidelines from Marvel Comics. He spent every weekend drawing furiously and eventually sent lots of art samples to the editors. Sometimes he'd hear back from an editor, and he was excited about that even if it was critical feedback. The fact that someone was reviewing his work was all he wanted. It helped spur him to keep drawing. It was a small step, but a step in the right direction.

Comic-Con draws celebrities, movie companies, publishers and, of course, comics artists from around the world. One report says that the con has an impact of over $162 million on the local San Diego economy.

PORTFOLIO REVIEW

If you're at that point where a critique of your work will assist in moving you to the next level as an artist, you may want to save up some money to attend a comic book convention, often abbreviated to *con*. I hope there is one relatively close to you. Check the websites in chapter 11: Resources for more info. Cons are everywhere on planet Earth, from Boston to Tokyo.

The San Diego Comic-Con, one of my favorites, is usually held in July or August. Editors—and even some selfless artists willing to help the next generation—do portfolio reviews with new talent. Most conventions have these reviews, but contact the con before you plan your trip.

Each editor or reviewer looks for different styles and ideas. Below is some advice on how to present yourself and your work, what editors want to see from you, and what you can expect from the portfolio review experience.

Be professional: Your review starts before the editor looks at your portfolio. When you're standing in line, don't brag about how good you are. Don't insult anyone else's work. Editors shouldn't judge you on what you wear, what kinds of comics you like, or where you're from, so don't throw a bad vibe their way either. Most important, be yourself. Relax. Listen to others' guidance.

Be organized: What do you want to show an editor? Organize your presentation beforehand. Don't shuffle through pages during your review, and be prepared to answer any questions the editor might have about your work. Invest in a quality portfolio folder, if possible. This isn't the time to pull creased and crinkled art samples out of a shopping bag.

Show your comics: Most editors want to see sequential art and aren't as interested in cover art, single illustrations, paintings, or sketches. They want to see if you can tell a story on a comics page. If an editor asks to see that other work, then you can show it. Show only your best and most current comics work, not all of your work. Focus on what best represents you right then.

Listen: You may have to wait in line for a while before your work is reviewed, so once you're up to bat, make the most of it. Listen to what the editors have to say. You don't have to follow all of their direction, but hear them out. They're there to help you, and, chances are, they'll give you useful advice to get you to the next stage.

What to expect: Don't assume you'll be hired on to *Iron Man* or *Green Lantern*, or be given your own project. You're really there for feedback. But you have every right to expect a focused, professional editor who will give you specific guidance to improve your comics. Take in all the sights of the show, meet with other creators like yourself, and see your favorite artists in person. It can be a great experience to be surrounded by hundreds of other people who enjoy comics as much as you do. It's all about learning the customs and culture of the comics industry.

Have fun: Of course! Let the comics fan side of you have a blast, too. It's the fan side that will remind you how much you love comics. That's going to help you achieve your goals.

(Hey, it worked for me. I'm living proof.) Enjoy yourself and revel in the experience of sharing your work with comics peers.

SUBMISSIONS GUIDELINES

If you can't make it to a comics convention, you can always submit your work to publishing companies through the mail. It's important to know that each company has specific submission guidelines. Most companies post that information on their websites. If they don't "officially" accept submissions, nothing's stopping you from being resourceful and sending them an introductory postcard with a sketch and your contact information on it. You might meet them at the next con, strike up a conversation, and make a solid connection to someone that shares your passion.

If you're aiming to be hired or commissioned by a company, remember that it takes time. Artists are showing different editors at different companies their work all the time. It might be months or years until you get your big shot. In all that time, never stop perfecting your art and refining your storytelling. Eventually, someone is going to believe in you. It's new talent like you that keeps the comics biz alive.

MIKE KUNKEL

From: Los Angeles, California
Job: Story artist and character designer in animation industry and comic book artist and writer
His Comics: *Herobear and the Kid, The Land of Sokmunster, Billy Batson and the Magic of Shazam!, Archie Babies, X-Men Unlimited #37, Superman/Batman #26*

Herobear and the Kid © Mike Kunkel

What was your first or favorite comic when you were younger?

The very first comic book I ever bought was *Flash* #308. I loved it! It had the Flash and a kid's adventure. It was great. But most of all, my favorite character growing up has always been Spider-Man. Always. Halloween costumes, sketches, comics, mail-away web-shooters. Always Spidey. Very close seconds have been Captain America, Booster Gold and Blue Beetle (in Maguire and Giffen's *Justice League*), Batman, and Captain Marvel. I always would grab a comic here and there, but when I seriously got into collecting comics, it was *Web of Spiderman* #18 that started me back in. Then, since I didn't have a comic shop by my house at the time, I would ride to every 7-Eleven and little Thrifty's store I could to search out old and current comics.

When did you know you wanted to make comics?

Always! Ha-ha! I have wanted to be a cartoonist since as far back as I can remember. In junior high and high school I drew my own comic strips and comic books, created my own characters and stapled little books together, and printed up little newsletters with my comic strips and stories. I've always wanted to write and draw cartoons.

What kinds of things inspire your comic book creations?

Inspiration can come from a lot of different areas . . . music, traveling somewhere new, old toys, watching old movies . . . And, often, it's spending time with my kids and remembering the adventures of childhood.

What tools do you use to create your comics?

First and foremost, I still just love pencil and paper. So pure and traditional! Now officially, it can depend on the project and process I'm looking for. For projects that I like to have originals [of] and work traditionally, I do all the work with Sanford Design Ebony pencils and sometimes Prismacolor pencils, and either smooth animation paper or cold-press Bristol board. Sometimes I'll even use vellum paper because I like how it takes the pencil for shading. For other projects that I work digitally, I'll use my Wacom Cintiq monitor, iPad, and a Toshiba Tablet PC. Scanning in roughs sometimes or creating them on the computer. Mostly working in SketchBook Pro and Photoshop for finished work. ArtRage is another fun program to work in.

What are great ways for kids to create comics right now?

Oh, there are so many fun ways for kids to create their own comics today! Using an iPad you can use Comic Life app to lay out your panels quickly and easily. Books can be printed a lot easier today. Online comics can be done digitally and quickly uploaded to a blog, website, or Facebook page to begin to build a following. Kids and kids at heart have a ton of opportunities and avenues to see their stories in tangible finished form—they just have to sit down and start working on them.

How do you use technology to create comics?

Using a Wacom Cintiq and a Toshiba Tablet PC, I can get a lot done. They allow me to achieve fun finished artwork that is readily available to share. I'll also use my iPad to sometimes rough out work when I'm traveling and working mobile.

Why is telling a story with comics important to you?

Telling stories with pictures and cartoons is so amazing and fun. People can pick up a book and instantly be transported to your world and characters. Comics are a very inviting medium that welcomes readers to jump into an adventure and read the pictures and stories together. For me, I always have and I always will want to tell stories visually.

How do you use social media to create or promote your work?

I'm behind in a lot of this. I really only use a blog and website. I'm not on any social networks. I have lots of friends trying to convince me to join them, but for me it seems like it would become more of a distraction. But eventually I'm sure I'll find the right way to use it for my projects and for what I'm after.

How does working on comics help you in other creative jobs?

Comics always help the fun of visual storytelling and cross over nicely with the other work that I do in animation. It also gives me an outlet to work on my own creative projects that I can share in other creative jobs.

THE BIZ

Just as each company has different guidelines on what it looks for in a new artist or project, each also has different terms on which it'll hire you or publish your work. Many companies use terms you might not have heard before, so here's a crash course on some basics that will help.

Contract: A contract is a legally binding document that you and the publisher sign, showing that you've both come to an agreement on what you'll produce and what he'll publish. There's a lot of information in a contract, so when you get to this stage, you'll definitely want a lawyer to look at it with you. There's not really such a thing as "fair" or "standard" when it comes to a contract—it's just whatever you and the company agree to do. If you feel you're being treated unfairly, respectfully say so. Remember that you have the power to negotiate. If you have access to affordable legal advice, this would be the time to use it.

> According to CBS News, Spider-Man and Wolverine are popular choices for kids' Halloween costumes, right up there with soldiers and firefighters.

Work for hire: Most popular comics, such as *The Hulk* and *The Flash* are done as work for hire. That means the artists are being hired to draw for an existing comic that the company owns or is licensing (for example, Dark Horse licenses *Star Wars* from Lucasfilm). You will be paid for your work, but you won't own what you create. However, you should have every right to keep your original art. Make sure that's part of the deal.

Creator owned: If something is creator owned, it means that you retain the copyright. That's just a fancy way of saying no one can do anything with your comic unless you legally let them, whether you publish it yourself or have someone else do it. For example, Bryan Lee O'Malley owns the copyright of *Scott Pilgrim*, but it's published by Oni Press. I own the copyright of *Nevermen*, but it was published by Dark Horse Comics, Inc.

Vouchers: At most companies, you submit a voucher for your work once it's completed. When you finish drawing an issue of *X-Men*, you send a voucher (a slip of paper with payment info, like an invoice) to your editor, letting him know how many pages you did and what to pay you. Depending on the contract, you might get a check right away, in thirty days, or when the book is published. It all depends, so read your contract before you sign it. It might affect your pay schedule.

Page rate: When you work on a comic, you get money for every page you do. This is determined before you start working, and it's stated in your contract. Page rates vary widely, depending on the book. You might get $150 to $200 just to pencil a comics page of *Superman*. You might get more, especially if you've become famous and you're an in-demand talent. On creator-owned projects, you might get a lot less money, but you keep ownership of what you create. For some artists, that's enough.

Royalty: No, not kings and queens. It means that in addition to getting a page rate, you might get some money later if the book you work on sells really well. If a book makes $100 profit, you might get $1, $10, or more, depending on the percentage in your contract. You usually get a royalty *after* the publisher has recouped some of what it spent to make your book.

Learn the ins and outs of contracts at some point. Don't let yourself be intimidated by them. It's important stuff to learn. It's part of the process once you become the artist on your favorite title, or on your very own creation. Contracts are part of the business once you're a pro. They help ensure your interests and the publisher's interests are met. You'll feel good when you know that in the world of contracts, *net* is not something to catch butterflies, and *gross* is not your baby sister's diaper.

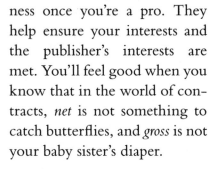

Plastic Man, made famous by artist Jack Cole, is one of a handful of offbeat protagonists. Other classics include Flaming Carrot, Gnatrat, The Tick, Sky Ape, and of course the legendary Teenage Mutant Ninja Turtles.

THE SHOW

In baseball, the triple-A teams call the major leagues The Show. I think that's a good metaphor for making it big in comics, too. If you have your sights set high, then that's the goal. At some point, your comics art and story should be ready to be reviewed by editors and publishers at comics companies. Maybe you'll be the next artist on *Spider-Man* or *Star Wars*. Maybe you'll get to create your very own comic with characters you designed and stories you wrote, like many of the artists profiled in this book. Prove that you can make great comics on your *own*, and be confident when you show your work to others. Use productive feedback to make your work better. A publisher might not have work for you right away. That's okay, and not something to discourage you. Remember, it's your love of comics that got you this far. Enjoy every stage of success, and keep doing those little things today that put you in a good position for tomorrow.

WILLIAM CHEN

Age: 11
Education: Fifth-grade student
His Comic: *Seeking a Strategy*

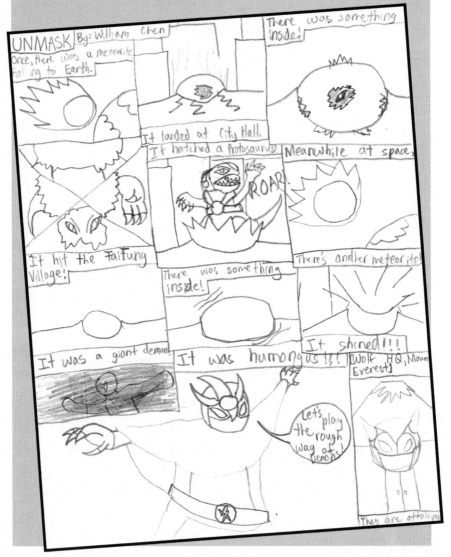

What are your favorite comic books?

LEGO Club Magazines because they have different comics that grabbed my attention.

Why do you like creating comics?

Art is my favorite subject. Also, I like to be creative because it expresses my feelings.

Where do you get the inspiration for your creations?
From class.

What are your favorite tools to use when writing and drawing comics?
I would use a pencil, paper, ruler, and my thinking cap.

Does technology help you create?
No. I sometimes use [a computer] for typing, but not for creating.

How do you think making comics could help you in other creative careers?
My future job is to be an artist. And I want to sell my art and raise money for making homes and other things to help people.

What's the best advice you can give your peers?
I'll say to be creative so that you can try to express yourself when you're creating drawings or comics.

BEYOND
COMIC BOOKS

Ever wonder what's beyond comics? Comic books are the center of the creative universe for a legion of talented directors, artists, musicians, writers, producers, video game designers, and animators. They've learned what you already know: there's something magical in comics that crosses all boundaries and is governed only by your imagination. Comics connect to more creative careers than you may have realized.

THE COMICS SQUAD

Many comic book companies divide the work for creating a comic book into more specialized positions. If you find yourself attracted to the comics world but find that you don't necessarily want to write, color, or draw, remember that there are lots of important production people behind the scenes that you rarely hear about. The artists and creators are just a part of a whole studio of talented people. Here are a few more specialized jobs in comics.

Creator: Comic book creators come up with the idea or concept behind the comic book. They may or may not do all the art or writing, but they are the ones with the creative vision behind the comic. Mike Mignola is the creator of *Hellboy*. He writes, draws, and owns it. Jerry Siegel and Joe Shuster created *Superman*, but lots of artists have worked on it, and DC Comics owns it. Marjorie Henderson Buell created Little Lulu as comics. Machiko Hasegawa created the *Sazae-san* manga. Other people worked on those characters when they became cartoons and merchandise.

Comics are a wellspring for Hollywood. *X-Men*, *Spider-Man*, and *Batman* have spawned sequels. Comics have attracted top-notch directors like Bryan Singer, Sam Raimi, and Chris Nolan.

Writer: Writers come up with the story and the script for the comic. They break the story down by panel for the artists. The writers are responsible for creating the scene description and dialogue, pretty much like film writers do for a movie script. Some pro comics writers include Alan Moore, Geoff Johns, Shaenon K. Garrity, Alan Grant, Grant Morrison, and Ann Nocenti.

Penciler: Pencilers draw the comic, but only in pencil. They begin by sketching thumbnails that follow the comic script, leaving extra room in each panel for the text. Then pencilers draw the final penciled illustrations on Bristol board. Some pro pencilers include Jon Bogdanove, Steve Pugh, Gene Ha, Ed McGuiness, and the groundbreaking Magnificent 24s group of Japanese female mangaka.

Inker: Inkers use brushes, crow quills, or Pigma pens to go over the pencilers' pages in black ink. This makes the page easier to reproduce into a finished comic. Some pro inkers include Kevin Nowlan, Terry Austin, Joe Sinnott, Klaus Janson, and John Severin.

Letterer: Letterers draw the word balloons, captions, and text. This is usually done between the pencil and ink stages. They use rulers to measure the letters so that they are all the same height. Lettering is almost always done by computer programs now, but small-press, indie creators like Craig Thompson still like to letter by hand.

Colorist: After the comic is inked, the art is scanned and color is added using computer software programs like Adobe Photoshop. Some colorists still use paints to color the comics, but this is becoming less common. Colorists like Dan Jackson, Pamela Rambo, Aron Lusen, and Dave Stewart color on computer, but still need knowledge of color theory.

Editor: Editors guide the entire process of creating the comic, from the work of the creators to proofreading the writer's words, as well as working closely with the pencilers, inkers, letterers, and colorists. There's no one exactly like a comic book editor. They are there at every stage, working with the writers and artists. They coordinate with the publisher, art director, and marketing people, too. Yet the best editor's hand is invisible, like a coach who trains her players, then lets them shine.

COOL COMICS-RELATED JOBS

If you like comics, you don't have to limit yourself to jobs in the comic book industry. Comics can give you a foundation for other forms of creativity. You could design video games, write for television, work on a movie, direct a music video, or produce an animated series. After being a comics editor, I worked as a producer for animated commercials, and almost wrote for a pro-wrestling company. (They thought comics were close to their storytelling, I guess.)

Here are just a few of the comics-related jobs out there:

Video game developer: Imagine working on the latest game for Nintendo or Playstation. That's what video game developers do—they work as programmers, animators, art directors, and video game testers, people whose job it is to test for glitches in game play. Your ability to draw comics can translate into the 3-D world of computer games. The UDON guys interviewed in this book work for Capcom, owner of the *Street Fighter* and *MegaMan* properties. Maybe you'll end up working for Rovio, and using your comics know-how to inspire the next *Angry Birds* phenomenon.

COMICS CREATOR

ART BALTAZAR

From: Chicago, Illinois
Job: Full-time famous cartoonist
His Comics: *Patrick the Wolf Boy*, Disney's *Gorilla Gorilla*, DC Comic's *Tiny Titans*, DC *Super Pets*, *Billy Batson and the Magic of Shazam!*, *Young Justice*, and upcoming Green Lantern adventures. By the way, Art is a *New York Times* bestselling author, two-time Eisner Award winner, and Harvey Award winner.

Patrick the Wolf Boy © Art Baltazar

Patrick the Wolf Boy © Art Baltazar

What was your first or favorite comic when you were younger?

The first comic I read was the one where Spider-Man got cloned from the Jackal, then scratched by Jackal's claw, then got a table thrown on him, and then got tossed down a chimney! It was awesome! I was around six years old, and I loved it! I also read anything with the Hulk and Superman.

When did you know you wanted to make comics?

I knew right after I read my first Spider-Man comic that I wanted to draw comics and cartoons and make up characters for the rest of my life. So far, so good!

What kinds of things inspire your comic book creations?

Everything! Life around me inspires me. Stories from everyday life. My kids. My family. Things I see. Life itself.

What tools do you use to create your comics?

I love drawing with pencils and ink and paper. I was trained traditionally. Recently, I started working digitally on a Cintiq [Wacom's interactive pen display], which is very awesome and saves tons of time!

What are great ways for kids to create comics right now?

Draw all the time, every day. Write down all your ideas, and buy a sketchbook! Draw in it all the time. Make things up. Tell stories. Write 'em down, and let your friends read your stuff. Oh yeah, and draw all the time.

How do you use technology to create comics?

I use my Cintiq to draw directly on the screen every day. I make comics 100 percent digital these days, and it rocks. Email comes in pretty handy to send my work to DC Comics.

Why is telling a story with comics important to you?

I think it's the best way to tell a story using words and visuals—besides movies and cartoons. But lots of movies start out as comics. I think it's the best because I have been reading stories this way since I was six years old. I have been making comics since 1992. Aw yeah, Famous Cartoonist!

How do you use social media to create or promote your work?

I use it all! The internet rocks, and is a great outlet for the world to see and read my comics. Go to www.artbaltazar.com. Aw yeah!

Production artist: Visualize being behind the scenes of your favorite movie or designing some of the characters in the movie. You can use what you've learned as a comic book artist and apply it to a creative job in movies. Brian O'Connell and Derek Thompson got to live the dream when they got to work on an *Aliens vs. Predator* comic. Then, they used their comics skills to become production artists. Now Brian works at Lucasfilm and Derek works at Pixar with other comics-inspired artists.

> Lots of famous people love comics. Actor Will Smith is a fan of *Akira*. Pro-wrestler CM Punk digs Marvel Comics. KISS front man Gene Simmons knows his comics trivia. Comedian Jerry Seinfeld is a Superman nut, and Shaquille O'Neal, a member of the NBA's 50 Greatest Players, has the Man of Steel's logo tattooed on his arm.

Children's book artist: Kids' picture books are like comics' cousins. They rely on both words and pictures to tell the story in sequence. The art is like big panels without word balloons. Some comics artists that dabble in picture books include Kellie Strom (*Sadie the Air Mail Pilot*), Rhode Montijo (*Cloud Boy/ Niño Nube*), and Jon Muth (*The Three Questions*).

Some artists are "triple threats." Hong Kong–born Alina Chau does her *Minty* comics, drew my *Treehouse Heroes* kids' book, and animates at Lucasfilm on *Clone Wars*. Joe Chiodo did *The Mechanic* comic, designed games for Digital Anvil and Electronic Arts, and illustrated *The Adventures of WonderBaby* kids' book.

Scriptwriter: Scriptwriters work in a variety of media. You can write screenplays for movies, as well as teleplays for television shows, including animated series. You can even create the story for video games. Screenplays and teleplays are very similar to comics scripts, so if you're writing for your own comic, you already have a good idea of how to write scripts in general. Frank Miller, who rejuvenated *Daredevil* and *Batman*, wrote for the *RoboCop* movies, and then went on to direct movies like *The Spirit*.

Crossovers are a comics phenomenon. Superman has faced Spider-Man. Batman has tested The Hulk. The X-Men met the Teen Titans. The Punisher has even met Jughead and the Archie gang. That was a strange day in Riverdale.

Cartoon creator: This is a description more than a job title. Cartoon creators come up with an idea for a cartoon based on their comics work and then stick around to help produce, design, or draw it. Comics artist Matt Groening, author of the comic *Life in Hell*, came up with television mainstay, *The Simpsons*. He's come a long way from doodles of rabbits named Binky and Bongo. Four comics book artists are behind Man of Action, and that studio created popular cartoons *Ben 10* and *Generator Rex*.

Storyboard artist: Storyboard artists are an unseen, but a very important, part of the filmmaking process. These artists are the ones working with the director to pace out the entire film, television show, or animated series in scene-by-scene drawings. Storyboards show setting, the placement of characters, and the main conflicts, actions, and resolves. Chances are whatever your favorite movie or cartoon is, there's a talented storyboard artist behind it, like Brandon Vietti. His credits include *Justice League: Crisis on Two Earths*, *Green Lantern: First Flight*, *Wonder Woman*, *Thor: Tales of Asgard*, *Planet Hulk*, *The Invincible Iron Man*, and *Batman/Superman Adventures*.

PHIL: Hey, Brandon, how did making comics prepare you for a job in animation?

BRANDON: The art of storytelling in comics is very similar to storytelling in film. They're both about communicating information with pictures. Comics use far fewer pictures than film, which is a great way to learn storytelling. Having fewer images to communicate with forces you to learn how to pick only the most important images for storytelling, and how to make those images have as much impact as possible. So, my earliest lessons in comic book storytelling are an important influence on my filmmaking decisions in animation today.

Film director: A director is the person with the unifying vision behind a film. The actors, production designers, costume designers, editors, and pretty much everyone else involved with the creative aspects of the movie take their cues from the director. The result is the vision you see on the screen. Before iconic director Hayao Miyazaki delighted international movies audiences, he drew manga, including the comics version of his anime, *Nausicaa*.

Comics publisher: A comics publisher is the person commissioning the line of cool comics you see on the shelf of your favorite comics store. If DC Comics is publishing a new series or Marvel is developing new characters, the publisher is involved. Mike Richardson started Dark Horse Comics. Though Dark Horse now makes movies and toys, too, comics are still essential, and Mike is there steering the ship. Another is Jim Lee, who cut his teeth as a Marvel artist and went on to helm a company called WildStorm Productions, which then became a DC Comics imprint.

Toy creator: Just like there are comic book conventions, there're also events like Toy Fair and DesignerCon, where companies and manufacturers of every size show what they do. Some comics artists find out they're so good at designing characters that they'd also be able to make cool toys. That's what the Muttpop guys did. They do their *Lucha Libre* comic, and make cool toys of their characters, too. *Teen Titans* artist Sean Galloway makes toys as well. From Hasbro to Bandai and everywhere in between, the toy world is a pretty awesome canvas for comic book artists, and worth exploring.

There's no one simple way to get a job as a storyboard artist for a big movie or as a designer for a video game company. The best thing to do, when you're ready, is to write those companies letters or send them emails, and ask them what you can do to prepare for that career. Really, the best question is, "How do I start?" Someday, maybe Marvel, DC Comics, DreamWorks, Lucasfilm, or Nintendo will be calling *you*.

YOUR LIFE AS A COMIC BOOK ARTIST

So, you want to be a comic book artist? Guess what? You already are. If you want to draw comics simply for your own pleasure, that can be very satisfying. If you want to go on to become a professional and get paid to do something you love, that's great, too. It's all up to you. In this book, you've discovered some tips on how to start a studio, write stellar stories, create fascinating characters, and show your work to the world. It's a good foundation to get you creating the best comic books you can. Flex your comics muscles. The more you use them, the stronger your comics will be.

AARON MOY

Age: 9
Education: Fourth-grade student
His Comic: *My Hero*

What are your favorite comic books?

My favorite is *Scooby-Doo* because it is funny.

Why do you like creating comics?

They are fun, and it passes the time.

What are your favorite tools to use when writing and drawing comics?

Pencils and crayons.

Does technology help you create?

I don't use technology—I just use paper.

How do you think making comics could help you with other creative careers?

I will become a better writer.

What are your plans for the future?

I want to write longer stories and show them to more of my friends.

What's the best advice you can give your peers?

Don't give up and keep on going!

RESOURCES: RECOMMENDED INDUSTRY INFO

KNOW THE COMIC BOOK PUBLISHERS

antarctic-press.com
archaia.com
archiecomics.com
boom-studios.com
darkhorse.com
dccomics.com
dccomics.com/mad
diamondcomics.com
drawnandquarterly.com
dynamite.net
editions-delcourt.fr

fantagraphics.com
firstsecondbooks.com
gomanga.com
idwpublishing.com
imagecomics.com
indyworld.com
kingfeatures.com/comics/comics-a-z
kodansha-intl.com/categories/manga-graphic-novels
marvel.com
onipress.com
platinumstudios.com
randomhouse.com/pantheon/graphicnovels
shogakukan.co.jp/company/english
shueisha.co.jp/english
toon-books.com/index2.php
topcow.com
topshelfcomix.com
tugboatpress.com
viz.com

VASILIS LOLOS

From: Athens, Greece
Job: Artist
His Comics: *The Last Call, The Pirates of Coney Island, Pixu, Hats*

What was your first or favorite comic when you were younger?
My favorite book as a kid was *Mighty Mouse,* but when I was young I also liked *Orion* by Masamune Shirow.

When did you know you wanted to make comics?
Although I was kinda late to the ball, I started thinking about making comics

Last Call © Vasilis Lolos

seriously when I was sixteen, give or take, and I haven't looked back since. I realized that all I wanted to do is art and drawings.

What kinds of things inspire your comic book creations?
I find inspiration in music, art, music album covers, fashion, design, and anything outside the drawing desk; I try to keep my radar open.

What tools do you use to create your comics?
My weapons of choice are brush and ink. I use the computer to color and design. Recently I started using it to draw, too; it lacks grittiness but makes up with "fine tuning."

What are great ways for kids to create comics right now?
Get a piece of paper, pencil, and an idea for a story to communicate. Don't concern yourself with too much, just do it.

How do you use technology to create comics?
I find that using a pen tablet cuts a lot of corners, but it is very crucial to know how to use pen and paper. I like the idea of animated panels and colors that print can't get—computers are perfect for that.

Why is telling a story with comics important to you?
It's all about communication, I think, connecting with the great unknown. Who knows? Maybe a guy like you will read your story in 180 years and say, "That's how I see things too! Man, that Lolos guy was awesome." And, sitting from my floating head cyberstand, I'll say, "Thanks, dude." Haha.

How do you use social media to create or promote your work?
I try to make the most of it, but I don't always succeed. I can't keep up with updating all that stuff. I am into it and getting around the newest promo platform, but I am bad at keeping up. I just want to make art. If I had someone to deal with all that and I could just say "update this, post that," I'd be happy.

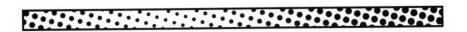

EXPLORE COMICS

collectmad.com

comicbookdb.com

comicbookgalaxy.com

comicbookresources.com

comicbookmovie.com

comiclist.com

comics.org

comicvine.com

comicsworthreading.com

comixology.com

coverbrowser.com

csnsider.com

deviantart.com

digitalcomicmuseum.com

freecomicbookday.com

garfieldminusgarfield.net

jmanga.com

kidjutsu.com

lambiek.net

livingbetweenwednesdays.com

mangafox.com

mangareader.net

mangastream.com

onemanga.com

popimage.com

sarjakuvaseura.fi

supermanhomepage.com

toonopedia.com

FIND COMICS LEGENDS

acmenoveltyarchive.org

acomics.com/best.htm

asterix.com

barnaclepress.com

bpib.com/illustra2/foster.htm

furinkan.com

www.george-herriman.com

julesfeiffer.com

kirbymuseum.org

micheleseworld.net/dmm/lulu/comics/comics.htm

muttscomics.com

peanuts.com

pogopossum.com

quino.com.ar

sergioaragones.com

tezukaosamu.net

thecarlbarksfanclub.com

us.tintin.com

tothfans.com

wallywoodart.blogspot.com

willeisner.com

LEARN MORE ABOUT THE ARTISTS IN THIS BOOK

PROFILED ARTISTS

Art Baltazar: artbaltazar.com

Sanford Greene: codegreene.blogspot.com

Mike Maihack: cowshell.com

Eleanor Davis: doing-fine.com

J. Bone: gobukan.blogspot.com

Sam Henderson: indyworld.com/Henderson

Rudy Spiessert: lekinorama.com/fiche_celebrite.
php?Ref=6224&DEssinateur=Rudy-Spiessert

Bryan Lee O'Malley: radiomaru.com; scottpilgrim.com

Mike Kunkel: theastonishfactory.com

UDON Entertainment: udonentertainment.com

Vasilis Lolos: steamrobo.blogspot.com;
www.vasilislolos.com

OTHER ARTISTS AND PROJECTS

andiwatson.biz
alinanimation.blogspot.com
aronlusen.com
brandonvietti.blogspot.com
derekmonster.com
dootdootgarden.com
gotcheeks.blogspot.com
koge.kokage.cc
maleev.com/DD
manofaction.tv
muttpop.com
popmhan.com
rhodemontijo.com
sadiethepilot.com
totoroforestproject.org

STUDY ART AND COMICS

academyart.edu
academy.smc.edu
afhboston.com
animation.filmtv.ucla.edu
artcenter.edu
calarts.edu
cartoonstudies.org
www.ccad.edu
dw-wp.com
interactive.usc.edu
kubertschool.edu
kyoto-seika.ac.jp/eng
massart.edu

mica.edu

parsons.edu

pratt.edu

risd.edu

saic.edu

scad.edu

schoolofvisualarts.edu

sheridancollege.ca

studiohijinx.com

teachingcomics.org

tomhart.net

uarts.edu

woodbury.edu

ATTEND A COMICS CONVENTION

www.ani-com.hk

baltimorecomiccon.com

bdangouleme.com

bostoncomiccon.com

comic-con.org

www.comiket.co.jp/index_e.html

conventionscene.com

dallascomiccon.com

designercon.com

emeraldcitycomicon.com

heroesonline.com/heroescon

kapowcomicconvention.com

kidscomiccon.com

komiks.dk

lehighvalleycomiccon.com

luccacomicsandgames.com

necac.net

newyorkcomiccon.com

oslocomicsexpo.no

www.planetcomicon.com
scenic-city.com/sfrg/calendar.htm
sicaf.org/2012/eng
spxpo.com
stumptowncomics.com
torontocomics.com
www.tokyoanime.jp/en
vancouvercomiccon.com

CHECK OUT A COMICS SHOP

comicopia.com
comicshoplocator.com
cosmicmonkeycomics.com
cybercitytoronto.tripod.com
beguiling.com
bigplanetcomics.com
bridgecitycomics.com
desertislandbrooklyn.com
isotopecomics.com
jhuniverse.com
www.kinokuniya.com
ekizo.mandarake.co.jp/shop/en/category-comic.html
meltcomics.com
themillionyearpicnic.com
thesecretheadquarters.com

VISIT COMICS ART MUSEUMS

carlemuseum.org
cartoonart.org
cartoonmuseum.org
comicscenter.net/en
geppismuseum.com
kyotomm.jp/english

moccany.org
tezukaosamu.net/en/museum

GET YOUR ART SUPPLIES

beepaper.com

canson-us.com

comicartistsupplies.com

crayola.com

dickblick.com

fabercastell.com

michaels.com

prismacolor.com

sakuraofamerica.com

strathmoreartist.com

utrechtart.com

winsornewton.com

EXPERIMENT ONLINE WITH ART AND COMICS

amazing-kids.org

artisancam.org.uk

bitstrips.com

comicmaster.org.uk

crayola.com/theartofchildhood/gallery/gallery.cfm

creativityforkids.com

donnayoung.org/art/comics.htm

google.com/doodle4google

goanimate.com

halfpixel.com

kidsbookshelf.com

makebeliefscomix.com

nga.gov/kids

pixton.com

superherosquad.marvel.com/create_your_own_comic

stripgenerator.com
toondoo.com
webcomics.com
wittycomics.com
wordle.net

HENRIK JONSSON

Age: 25
Education: Student at The Kubert School
His Comic: *The Norseman*

What are your favorite comic books?

I've always been a huge fan of characters like Captain Britain and Captain America. As a kid [growing up in Sweden] they were very foreign. Which was very interesting and exciting. I have a huge interest in history and mythology, so I tend to go for books like that. The Swedish magazine, *Magnum*, that reprinted Preacher and Judge Dredd was a life-changer back in the day, as well.

Why do you like creating comics?

I love drawing and art. Trying to make reality out of even the most outlandish and ridiculous story to make you feel and believe it, is such a satisfaction to me. It's the ability to give your imagination life and share it with others.

Where do you get the inspiration for your creations?

I find a lot of inspiration from mythology and history. Sometimes I'll read or hear about some current events that will either be really uplifting or [upset me] beyond belief. So [I find inspiration in] life in general most of the time. Usually I make a "soundtrack" to the story I'm drawing to get me in the right mood, too.

What are your favorite tools to use when writing and drawing comics?

For writing, a coffeepot, and for drawing, whatever gets the job done. I usually work with a lot of tracing paper to fix figures or better a composition. Raphael No. 1 brush is preferred for inking, and prior to that I use 2H pencils.

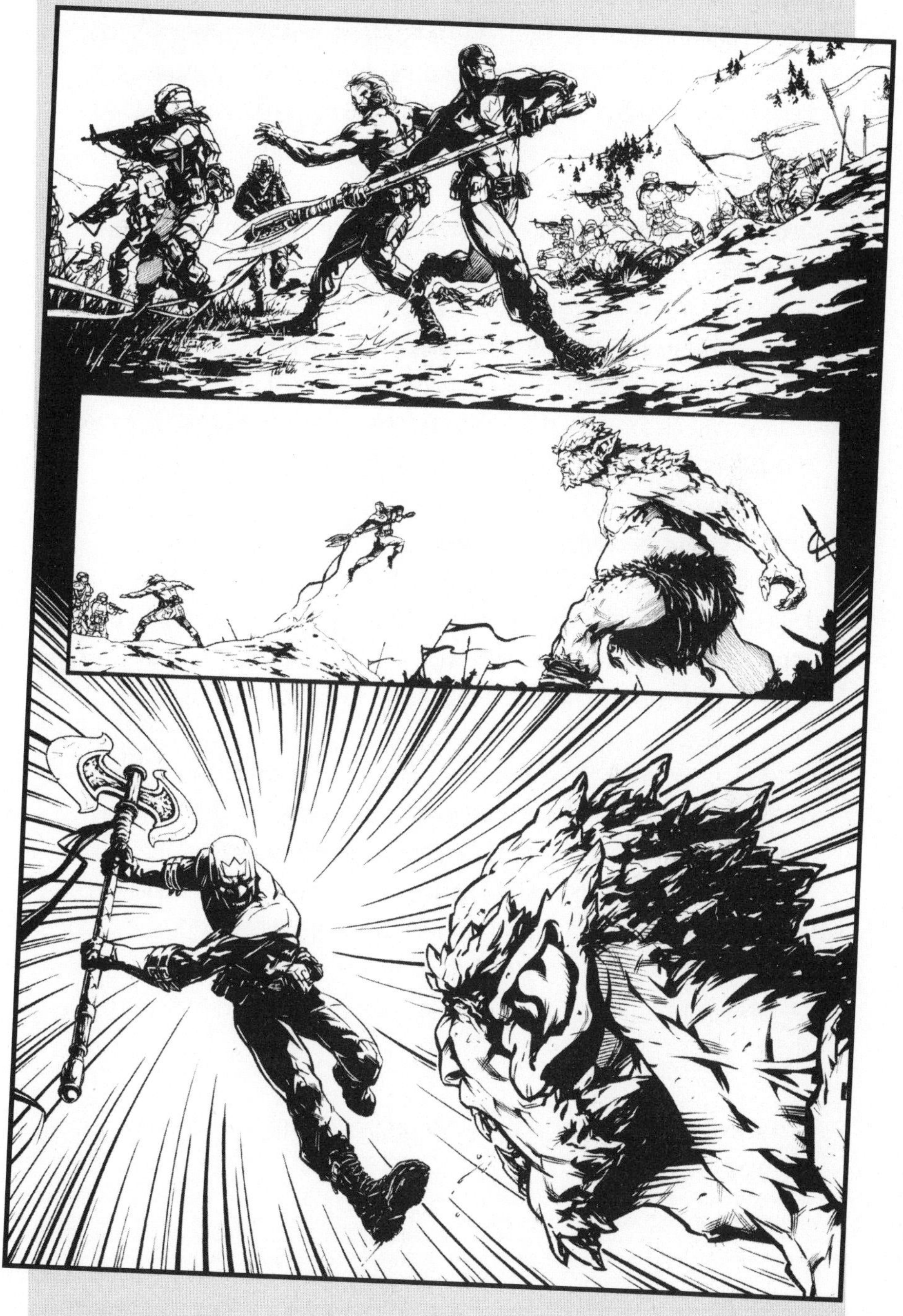

Does technology help you create?

I use a copy printer a lot to fix sizing issues. I also blue-line print my pencils to ink. If needed, I'll do paste-ups and touch-ups on the computer, but I prefer my art to be as traditional as possible. Painting portraits in Photoshop has proven to be a fun and relaxing change of pace sometimes, though.

How do you think making comics could help you in other creative careers?

By making comics, I understand storytelling more. It has definitely helped me with writing by being able to envision a story in more detail. Before The Kubert School, I took care of people living with severe autism, and we used pictures and sequential art to communicate, as actions being explained verbally often could be confusing and misunderstood.

What are your plans for the future?

Hopefully, having it become reality in print. *The Norseman* is basically me putting everything I love about comics and everything else into one cohesive story. Though honestly I just want a job drawing. My own personal comic is a fun hobby but won't pay for rent. I'd like to try and make that happen, though.

What's the best advice you can give your peers?

Keep working and never stop. I try to draw a sketch a day no matter what. When I have other artwork to do, I sketch as a warm-up. You should also be open and ask for criticism. That's how you learn to get better.

12

ESSENTIAL
COMIC BOOK
TERMINOLOGY

Now that you're familiar with most of the terms covered throughout the book, here are a few more, so you'll *really* know your stuff!

Anime [annie-MAY]: The Japanese word for *animation*. A widely popular style of Japanese animation, similar to the American cartoon, but having its own singular style and a wide range of subject matter.

Background: The setting of a story when it is actually drawn onto the comics page.

Balloons: The flat, bubble-like spaces with hooks, or tails, that contain the words the characters are speaking or thinking.

Bleed: A stylistic choice used by the artist to fill up the gutter, or white space around the panels, with art. Bleed art goes right to the edge of the page.

Character: A fictional person or creature portrayed in your comic, around whom the story is based.

Comic book: A sequence of art and words that tells a story and is typically bound into book or magazine form.

Comic strip: A series of art and words in short, horizontal format, generally three to eight panels.

Credits: The acknowledgement of the creative staff of a comic book, which is usually a list of names and respective jobs.

Graphic novel: A novel written in comic book format, usually one hundred pages or more, with a square binding.

Gutter: A thin strip of blank white space that runs between individual panels.

Inker: An artist who goes over the penciled page of comics art with a brush or an ink quill to enhance reproduction.

Letterer: A person who draws all the words of dialogue and sound effects in a comic book.

Manga [mahn-GAH]: The Japanese word for *comic book* or *graphic novel*, which is used in English to describe Japanese comic books or a style of comics art.

Panels: The blocks of art, usually framed, that make up a comic strip or book.

Penciler: An artist who draws a comic book only in pencil.

Printing: The process of producing printed material by ink or press. Printing takes original comic book art to its published comic book form.

Spine (binding): The folded or hinged back of a book that holds its pages together. A spine can be stapled, sewn, or glued.

Title: Also known as a header or logo, the title is the name of a comic book. The logo is another name for the title in its official, designed form.

Theme: The underlying subtext behind the telling of a story.

Writer: A person who writes the script that a comic book artist follows when drawing the pages.

CONTRIBUTING ARTISTS

Thank you to all the artists who agreed to be profiled and who contributed their wonderful artwork.

Art Baltazar

Patrick the Wolf Boy © Art Baltazar

J. Bone and J. Torres

Alison Dare © J. Bone and J. Torres, published by Tundra books, 2010

Eleanor Davis

Secret Science Alliance and The Copycat Crook © Eleanor Davis

Sanford Greene

Rotten Apple © Sanford Greene

Sam Henderson

"Scene But Not Heard" (from *Nickelodeon Magazine*) © Sam Henderson

Mike Kunkel

Herobear and the Kid © 2012 Mike Kunkel

Bryan Lee O'Malley

Scott Pilgrim © Bryan Lee O'Malley
Kim Pine © Bryan Lee O'Malley

Vasilis Lolos

Last Call © Vasilis Lolos

Mike Maihack	*Cleopatra in Space* © Mike Maihack
Rudy Spiessert	*Ooga-Booga* © Rudy Spiessert
UDON Entertainment	*Street Fighter Legends: Ibuki* Story by Jim Zub, Art by Omar Dogan, Published by UDON Entertainment Street Fighter © CAPCOM - All rights reserved
William Chen	*Seeking a Strategy* © 2011 William Chen
Alexis Cornell	© 2011 Alexis Cornell
Angela Fernot	*Legends of the Owl Queen* © 2011 Angela Fernot
Henrik Jonsson	*The Norseman* © 2011 Henrik Jonsson
Masina Kim	*Suki N. Moss and the Spaceship* © 2011 Masina Kim
Justin Lee	*Armortek* © 2011 Justin Lee
Aaron Moy	*My Hero* © 2011 Aaron Moy
Evan Okui	*Silver Shadow* © 2011 Evan Okui
Wesley St. Claire	*Nasser of Aban* © 2011 Wesley St. Claire
Edward Sullivan	*Big Bot* © 2011 Edward Sullivan
Saratep Suthy	*EviL Love LivE* © 2011 Saratep Suthy

A special thanks to J. Bone for the awesome cover
illustrations as well as the spot art found
on pages i, v, vii, viii, ix, and xi.